How to use Differentiation in the Classroom:

The Complete Guide

By Mike Gershon

Series Introduction

The 'How to...' series developed out of Mike Gershon's desire to share great classroom practice with teachers around the world. He wanted to put together a collection of books which would help professionals no matter what age group or subject they were teaching.

Each volume focuses on a different element of classroom practice and each is overflowing with brilliant, practical strategies, techniques and activities – all of which are clearly explained and ready-to-use. In most cases, the ideas can be applied immediately, helping teachers not only to teach better but to save time as well.

All of the books have been designed to help teachers. Each one goes out of its way to make educators' lives easier and their lessons even more engaging, inspiring and successful then they already are.

In addition, the whole series is written from the perspective of a working teacher. It takes account of the realities of the classroom, blending theoretical insight with a relentlessly practical focus.

The 'How to...' series is great teaching made easy.

Author Introduction

Mike Gershon has been creating resources for teachers since 2009. His twenty guides to classroom practice have been viewed and downloaded over 2.7 million times by teachers in more than 180 countries.

All Mike's resources can be downloaded for free at www.tes.co.uk/mikegershon

The TES (Times Educational Supplement) website is a wonderful platform providing user-generated content for teachers, by teachers. It is an online community of professionals which reaches into the heart of classrooms across the globe, bringing great resources to teachers and learners on every continent of the planet.

Having seen how his fellow professionals responded to his resources, Mike knew he had to go that one step further and provide book-length material that could help teaching and learning in classrooms throughout the world. And so, thanks in no small part to the fantastic platform provided by the TES, the 'How to...' series was born.

For more information on Mike, his books, training and consultancy, other writing and resources, visit www.mikegershon.com

Other Works from the Same Author

Available to buy now on Amazon:

How to use Differentiation in the Classroom: The Complete Guide

How to use Assessment for Learning in the Classroom: The Complete Guide

How to use Questioning in the Classroom: The Complete Guide

How to use Discussion in the Classroom: The Complete Guide

How to Teach EAL Students in the Classroom: The Complete Guide

More Secondary Starters and Plenaries

Secondary Starters and Plenaries: History

Teach Now! History: Becoming a Great History Teacher

The Growth Mindset Pocketbook (with Professor Barry Hymer)

Also available to buy now on Amazon, the entire 'Quick 50' Series:

50 Quick and Brilliant Teaching Ideas

50 Quick and Brilliant Teaching Techniques

50 Quick and Easy Lesson Activities

50 Quick Ways to Help Your Students Secure A and B Grades at GCSE

50 Quick Ways to Help Your Students Think, Learn, and Use Their Brains Brilliantly

50 Quick Ways to Motivate and Engage Your Students

50 Quick Ways to Outstanding Teaching

50 Quick Ways to Perfect Behaviour Management

50 Quick and Brilliant Teaching Games

50 Quick and Easy Ways to Outstanding Group Work

50 Quick and Easy Ways to Prepare for Ofsted

50 Quick and Easy Ways Leaders can Prepare for Ofsted

Acknowledgements

First and foremost I must thank Jeremy Hayward, who taught me to teach. He has been a major influence and he is, without doubt, the best teacher I know. Thanks also to the many great teachers I have had over the years, specifically Judith Schofield, Richard Murgatroyd, Simon Mason, Cath Nealon, Andrew Gilliland, Graham Ferguson, and Simon Ditchfield. I must also thank all the wonderful teachers I have worked with and learnt from at Central Foundation Girls' School, Nower Hill High School, Pimlico Academy and King Edward VI School, Bury St. Edmunds. Special mention must go to the Social Sciences team at Pimlico, to Jon Mason and to James Wright. Of course, I cannot fail to thank all the fantastic students I have had the pleasure of teaching – particularly all the members of HC and HD at Pimlico. In addition, I am greatly indebted to the people I trained with at the IOE and, in particular, to Erin, Liam, Anna and Rahwa. Finally, thanks to my mum for her unfailing support over the years and her wonderful example.

I have picked up many of the activities, strategies and techniques in this book from the countless wonderful people I have worked with, however, any errors or omissions remain my own.

Table of Contents

Chapter One – Introduction

Welcome to *How to Use Differentiation in the Classroom.* Contained within is a wealth of practical ideas which teachers can pick up and begin using immediately, no matter what age group they teach, or what area of the curriculum they specialise in.

This is a book which will help you to improve your own classroom practice, as well as the learning experience of your students.

Everything has been written with the busy teacher in mind. The strategies, techniques and activities which follow are all ready-to-use and take account of the practicalities of day-to-day teaching.

This is a book which will help you to be a brilliant teacher.

It is a book which will help you to raise achievement.

It is a book that will help you make your classroom an engaging, motivational environment in which learning is at the top of everyone's agenda.

In chapters two to six, one hundred different differentiation strategies, activities and techniques are outlined and explained. In addition, it is made clear in each case why and how this leads to effective differentiation.

Therefore, through using this book you will not only get access to a huge range of differentiation methods, but you will also develop your understanding of what successful differentiation involves.

The chapters are divided as follows:

Chapter Two – Activities

Chapter Three – Questioning

Chapter Four – Things you can ask students to do or use

Chapter Five – Things the teacher can do

Chapter Six – Words and Writing

Chapter Seven – Conclusion

Everything in chapters two to six can be used across the curriculum and with a variety of age groups. The separate sections provide a way in which to divide the topic of differentiation up, making it more manageable for you, the teacher.

There are two ways in which you can use this book:

1) Read it from cover-to-cover. This will give you a deep insight into how successful differentiation works. It will also provide you with myriad ways through which to make this happen in your classroom.

2) Dip in and out. This will allow you to visit the sections which you feel are most relevant to your own classroom practice. It will mean that you are using the book like a compendium; taking from it whatever you feel is useful for your day-to-day planning and teaching.

Whichever approach you take, I know that you will find strategies, activities and techniques which will work for you and for your students. This, in turn, will help you to create great learning experiences and it will help your pupils to make significant progress.

Before moving onto practicalities, let us briefly consider what we mean by differentiation.

What is Differentiation?

Differentiation is simple. It involves planning and teaching in a way that takes account of all learners in a class. By working in this manner, teachers ensure that every student has the opportunity to make good progress, regardless of their starting point.

From this definition, you will note that differentiation actually encompasses a whole range of strategies, activities and techniques. It goes from talking to students, to eliciting information, to encouraging independence, to providing extension tasks, and much more besides.

Different circumstances will make different demands on the teacher. Therefore, to differentiate effectively, one needs to have a variety of methods on hand, ready to be deployed. That is what this book offers. One hundred of them. All ready-to-use. All clearly outlined and explained.

So, let's go and have a look at them.

Chapter Two – Activities

In this chapter we look at twenty-five brilliant activities which can be used to differentiate your lessons, no matter what subject you are teaching or what age-group.

1. Hot-Seating

What does it involve?

The 'hot-seat' is a chair at the front of the class in which students take it in turns to sit. While they are there, the rest of the class gets to ask them questions about the topic being studied. The student in the 'hot-seat' has to try and answer the questions, calling on their knowledge of the topic to do so. Two variations of the activity are as follows: First, ask the student who is in the 'hot-seat' to play a role. For example, if the topic was the life of Henry VIII, the student could take on the role of one of his wives. The student would then answer the questions 'in role'. Second, invite a team of students (between two and four) to take up the 'hot-seat'. They can then work together to answer the questions posed by the rest of the class.

How does it differentiate?

- All students are able to access the task. This is because everybody can ask questions of the student(s) in the 'hot-seat'. The only criteria which must be met are that the questions relate to the topic.
- Information about the topic is presented to students through the speech of their peers. This makes it easier for them to access the work and to engage with the knowledge and ideas in question.
- The task is dramatic. It is driven by a tension between the student(s) in the 'hot-seat' and the rest of the class. This stems from the fact that the class are asking questions of the

student(s) which they may or may not be able to answer – the tension comes from the ambiguity. In turn, this makes the task engaging for all students.

2. Socratic Dialogue

What does it involve?

A Socratic dialogue is a conversation between the teacher and one or two students. It involves the teacher using a combination of questions, arguments, counter-arguments, examples and counter-examples in order to challenge the thinking of the student(s) in question. The method stems from the character of Socrates in Plato's dialogues. In these texts, Socrates, a philosopher who lived in Athens in Ancient Greece, is presented as someone who challenges others to think about their own thinking. He does this by demonstrating inconsistencies in their thought and showing how assumptions by which they live and reason are not necessarily sound. Socrates' purpose for this was to get closer to truth, to cultivate wisdom and to encourage others to think critically about their own ideas, as well as about the society in which they lived.

Two uses of Socratic dialogue in the classroom are as follows: First, while students are engaged in a task, the teacher chooses a pupil and asks them to explain their thinking about the topic. A dialogue ensues in which the teacher challenges the pupil's ideas through the use of thoughtful questioning, the offering of alternative arguments and the suggestion of counter-examples. The point is not to prove the student wrong and the teacher right. It is to encourage the student to think more carefully, critically and clearly about their own ideas. Second, the teacher engages in a dialogue as described previously, except it is now treated as the main activity. The whole class listens in as the teacher discusses whatever is at issue with one or two students, in a Socratic manner. Other students might like to join in as the dialogue progresses.

How does it differentiate?

- In the first case, it provides a means whereby the teacher can provide personalised learning for one or two students at a time. The level of challenge the teacher puts into the dialogue can be tailored to the needs of the student(s).
- In the second case, it provides a means whereby the whole class can access a high level discussion concerned with the topic being studied (and the conceptual thinking which underlies that topic).
- In both cases, it causes students to think about their own thinking on the topic. This helps them to make progress, wherever they are at, because it is based on reviewing and refining the position at which they currently find themselves. In this sense, the learning is personalised.

3. Open Activities

What does it involve?

In many tasks, what it is that students are being asked to do is fairly circumscribed and specific. This is because the teacher is usually working from the premise that all students need to do whatever there is to be done, in order that the learning outcomes can be successfully met. This is a fair premise, but not one that leads by necessity to the conclusion – namely, that all pupils should do the same thing in the same way. The alternative is to make activities more open.

Open activities are those in which the teacher sets the guidelines but then leaves it for students to decide how to go about meeting them. Here are some examples:

- 'Here is a list of the things you must do. It is up to you how you go about doing them. The only rule is that you must be able to demonstrate your work to me.'

- Provide students with a question or statement and ask them to respond in a way they see fit (you might like to provide some ideas in case they get stuck).

- Tell students where they should be at the end of the lesson and then invite them to work out their own way of getting there (you will need to provide support to the least able students).

Clearly, such activities will not always be appropriate. It is undoubtedly the case that there are many times when closed activities are either preferable or necessary. However, building in a range of open activities to a programme of study can have a really positive effect on student engagement and progress.

How does it differentiate?

- Students are able to decide for themselves how they are to go about completing the task. This means that they can play to their own strengths – particularly if you have spent time getting them to think about how they learn best (which means they will be primed with the knowledge to make good choices).
- If an activity is left open then there are many ways in which a student might engage with it. If there are many options available, it means there is a higher likelihood that students will find an approach which suits them.
- The method encourages students to work independently and to have confidence in their own abilities. This is because the teacher is making it clear that they believe their pupils can work successfully within a set of general guidelines. If students have confidence in themselves, they are more likely to make progress regardless of their starting position.

4. Stepped Activities

What does it involve?

Let us imagine that you are planning a lesson. How are you going to ensure that all students are stretched and challenged throughout the session? One easy way in which to do this is through stepped activities. These are tasks which contain a series of separate elements, the difficulty level of which gradually increases. Here is an example:

Topic: Rainforests

Part 1: Write a letter to a friend explaining what rainforests are and where they are found.

Part 2: Draw a diagram showing how rainforests develop. Label your diagram and write an explanation next to it.

Part 3: Analyse Source B. How does the source relate to what you know about rainforests? What is the purpose of the source? What does the source not tell you?

Part 4: Create a table outlining three arguments in favour of deforestation and three arguments against deforestation.

Part 5: How might you create and police a successful system of regulation for protection of the rainforest in Brazil, given the limited resources available to the government (listed in Source C) and the previous attempts which have failed (explained in Source D)?

Each part of the activity is a little harder than that which came immediately before. This means that all students will be challenged throughout the task (and will, in turn, make progress). Those who are skilled in the subject will be able to reach and complete parts four and five. Those who are less able in the subject may instead get to part three. Both sets of students will be stretched by the task and neither will suffer the frustrations associated with finding the work too easy or too difficult to access.

How does it differentiate?

- The method results in activities which gradually increase in difficulty. This means that the ability levels of all students in a class are catered for.
- All students are challenged and all students are able to experience success. This is because the various 'steps' in the activity correlate to different levels of difficulty.
- The various 'steps' can involve a variety of activity types or approaches. This means that the teacher will be catering to the different strengths their students possess. It may be that Student A finds part two challenging because it involves a certain skill with which they have difficulty, but that part three then plays to one of their strengths (while stretching their thinking because of the increased sophistication of the content).

5. Options

What does it involve?

This entails providing students with a range of options from which they might choose in order to complete a task. For example, the teacher might give pupils a couple of questions or statements (or one of each) to which they are then to respond using two options from a list:

'The Charge of the Light Brigade is more about brutality than nobility'

'How does the poem make use of repetition?'

Respond to the question and the statement using any two of the following options:

- Write an essay.

- Create an extended cartoon strip.

- Make a poster advertising your answer.

- Write a poem.

- Come up with a short drama piece.

- Draft a speech in which you put forward your point of view.

- Create a radio interview focussing on either the question or the statement.

There are three ways through which you can vary this approach. First, you might like to divide the list of options into two or three categories and ask students to select one option from each in order to complete the task. By doing this, you can ensure that pupils produce responses that are suitably varied, or which are based on certain skills or ways of thinking.

Second, you might like to provide two questions, two statements, or a question and a statement, and ask students to select one of these to which they then respond using two different methods. The advantage of this approach is that pupils are caused to think about the same thing from alternative perspectives. This will help them to develop a broader understanding of that which is in question.

Third, ask your class to come up with what they think is a suitable range of options by which one might respond to the questions or statements. This would be in the form of a discussion in which students advocate for various methods, with a final list being decided upon through voting.

How does it differentiate?

- The approach presents students with a range of options from which they may choose. This means that the way in which the task is completed is up to them. As such, they can opt for methods with which they feel comfortable and which play to their strengths.

- The approach is based on the notion of students having a range of options from which to choose. There is thus less likelihood that there will be a student for whom no option provides a viable method.
- The teacher can select a list of options which vary in difficulty. This will mean that students can self-select in order to challenge themselves (perhaps with a little prompting from the teacher, or through splitting the options into 'easy' and 'hard' categories – with students having to pick one from each).

6. Choices

What does it involve?

Give students a range of questions or tasks and ask them to pick which ones they will deal with and in which order. The questions and tasks should be of varying levels of difficulty. You might want to present them in an order reflecting their difficulty levels, or you might prefer to jumble them up. The advantage of the latter approach is that students are less likely to go for the level they think they are at and more likely to choose questions or tasks which interest them. With that said, there will always be the possibility that some students will analyse any list with the express aim of identifying the items which appear to be the simplest or most straightforward.

Here is an example of the activity in practice:

Topic: Buddhism and the Four Noble Truths

Choose and complete two of the following:

- Draw a cartoon strip showing each of the four noble truths.
- Retell the story of how the Buddha came to understand the four noble truths.

- What are the similarities between Buddhism and two other religions?
- How might a Buddhist live according to the four noble truths in modern society?
- In what ways might the world be different if all of us lived our lives according to the four noble truths?

As you will note, the range of choices all connect to the topic and make differing demands of students. Two variations of the activity are as follows:

First, you may choose to have two categories (for example: tasks and questions; easy and hard; knowledge and understanding) and ask students to make one choice from each of these. Second, you may invite students to work in pairs and ask each member to make one choice. The pair then works together to complete the questions or tasks they have chosen.

How does it differentiate?

- The method allows students freedom and independence to make choices in accordance with what they feel they can do and where they feel they are at.
- It lessens the likelihood of students struggling to engage with the task (the range of choices means there are more chances that pupils will see something which they can access).
- The range of choices means that students are able to identify the possibilities which they believe will help them to make progress. This ensures the learning is personalised.

7. Group Work

What does it involve?

In general this involves students working together in groups of three or more in order to complete a task of some sort. It is advisable to keep groups smaller where possible (three or four students will suffice) as this prevents the possibility of certain group members becoming passengers (who sit back while the rest get on with the work). Here are some specific examples of group work:

- Students work together to produce something which could be done individually (for example, an essay).
- Students work together to produce something which could not be done individually (for example, a multi-person drama piece).
- Students work together to respond to some stimulus (for example, they investigate a problem which the teacher has presented to them).
- Students work together to share their thinking (for example, a discussion). This could be an end in itself, or a prelude to a further task (for example, the creation of a presentation).
- Students work together as part of a whole-class effort (for example, a task in which a member of each group acts as an envoy who goes off to teach their peers).

In each case, it is expected that students will produce their work in conjunction with one another. It may be that pupils work on different aspects of the task, but they will be doing so in the knowledge that their particular element will go to help form the whole.

How does it differentiate?

- If students work together in a group, they are able to apportion tasks based on the relative strengths of the group members. This means that pupils can focus on what they are good at, helping their group to succeed and ensuring that they personally engage with the task.

- Students working in a group are able to build and create knowledge and understanding together. This means that members of a group who are particularly able, or who know a lot about the matter in hand, are able to help others to learn who do not find themselves in such a position.
- Group work involves discussion. Pupils are likely to have a lot of experience talking with their peers. They will be able to call on this in their work-based discussion. In turn, this makes the task accessible.

8. Pair Work

What does it involve?

Pair work involves students working on a task with a partner. Here are some specific examples:

- The teacher introduces a piece of stimulus material and asks students to do something with this (analysis or evaluation, for example) while working in pairs.
- The teacher asks students to discuss a question or statement in pairs.
- The teacher gives students a task which could be done individually (for example, analysing a source) and asks students to complete this in pairs.
- The teacher gives students a task which could not be done individually (for example, interviewing) and asks students to complete this in pairs.
- The teacher gives students a task which will subsequently see them engaging with other students (for example, a snowballing task in which students first work in pairs and then move into fours).

Pair work has many benefits. Three of the most important are:

i.   It allows all students in a class to engage actively with the work.
ii.   It requires little preparation.
iii. It combines simply with a wide variety of other activities.

How does it differentiate?

- It gives all students the opportunity to engage with the work. This is because the whole class is divided into a series of mini-groups which are sufficiently small as to allow everybody the opportunity to take part.
- Through judicious seating arrangements, the teacher can create pairings that consist of students who can help one another to learn (for example, a more able student with a less able student).
- It provides a means whereby the teacher can visually identify who has not understood the work. This is achieved by observing the class as a whole and seeing which pairs are confused or are not working. The teacher can then focus on supporting these groups.

9. Discussion

What does it involve?

Discussion involves students talking and listening to one another. This will usually be underpinned by a purpose, for example: an attempt to answer a question; the exploration of a statement; the search for a solution to a problem.

A variety of discussion activities exist, see my book 'How to use Discussion in the Classroom' for detailed explanation of a large number of these. Broadly speaking, we can divide discussion activity types into three categories: whole-class discussion, paired discussion and group discussion. It is worth thinking briefly about each of these in turn.

Whole-class discussion involves everybody working together in order to share thoughts on a certain topic. It will normally be led by the teacher and will involve most of the class being silent and listening for most of the time. This is so that the person who is speaking has the opportunity to get their point across.

Paired discussion involves the class being divided into groupings of two. Each grouping (pair) discusses whatever it is that the teacher has indicated is at issue. The activity is started off by the teacher and then involves everybody in the classroom having the opportunity to talk and to listen. It creates a noisy, positive atmosphere which is often coupled with a string sense of participation.

Group discussion involves the class being divided into groupings of more than two. Each group discussed whatever it is that the teacher has indicated is at issue. The activity is started off and then monitored by the teacher. It is likely that some students will talk more than others, though each member of each group should have ample opportunity to share their thoughts. This is more likely to be the case if groups are kept to three or four in size.

How does it differentiate?

- Nearly all students will find speaking more straightforward than writing. Therefore, discussion activities are likely to engage all members of the class (or, at the least, make the lesson content more accessible).
- It is widely held that speech acts as a good precursor to writing because it helps you to get your own thoughts in order, thus making it easier to transfer them into the written word. Discussion activities therefore help make writing more accessible to all students.

- Talking means sharing that which is in your mind. Whatever the type of discussion used, it is likely that students will be exposed to ideas other than their own. There is therefore a high chance that pupils involved in discussion will see their understanding develop, regardless of the point at which they start.

10. Card Sorts

What does it involve?

Students are provided with a collection of cards relating to the topic. On each card there is a different piece of information. The teacher instructs students to do certain things with the cards. Examples of what this might include are:

- Discuss the cards which most interest you with a partner.
- Order the cards from most to least important.
- Categorise the cards.
- Match the cards.
- Connect the cards together in a map.

Pupils can work individually, in pairs or in groups. The second option is often the most successful. Here is a specific example of a card sort in order to demonstrate what has been said:

Topic: Human Rights

Students work in pairs. Each pair is given a set of cards containing the following human rights (one right per card): right to life; right not to be tortured; right to equality before the law; right to privacy; right to family life; right to move freely; right to a nationality; right to rest and leisure; right to work.

Students are asked to rank the cards from most to least important. They are instructed to discuss the various rights and to agree upon an order.

How does it differentiate?

- The use of cards means that students are provided with something tangible which they can hold and move. This contrasts with the abstract manipulation of ideas which takes place inside one's mind. As a result, the structure of the activity makes the content more accessible for students.
- Pupils are able to visualise their thinking. Taking the example from above, pairs could arrange the cards so as to reflect that which was in their mind. This, in turn, allows them to examine and analyse the contents of their mind more simply than would be the case if their thinking remained purely internal.
- Card sorts can be used as a precursor to other tasks, such as writing. This differentiates because it breaks up the thinking students have to do into discrete parts. This results in increased accessibility because pupils can attend to one process at a time.

11. Match Group Rank

What does it involve?

Matching involves students connecting together items that are similar or related. Grouping involves students bringing items into conjunction according to some set of criteria (for example, a category or a series of categories). Ranking involves placing items in an order relative to one another, with the order being predicated on some set of criteria. Here are three examples to demonstrate these points:

Matching:

Students are provided with a series of historical sources and a series of historical writers. Their task is to match the writer to the source.

Grouping:

Students are provided with a series of historical sources and a set of categories ('very trustworthy', 'quite trustworthy', and 'not trustworthy'. Their task is to group the sources according to the various categories.

Ranking:

Students are provided with a series of historical sources and a scale which ranges from 'very useful in answering the question' to 'not at all useful in answering the question.' Their task is to rank the sources in accordance with the scale.

In each of these cases, students would be expected to explain and justify the decisions they make.

How does it differentiate?

- The various tasks involve abstract thinking (justification) being accessed through concrete decision-making (matching, grouping and ranking).
- Each of the methods provides students with a set of criteria which they are to apply. This avoids the difficulties which can arise when criteria are left implicit or when knowledge of them is assumed.
- The level of justification which students give will be in accordance with where they are at in terms of their learning. This means all students can achieve success in the task but that more able students will still find themselves challenged.

12. Design Brief

What does it involve?

Students are provided with a design brief. It is up to them how they fulfil this. Here is an example:

Design Brief: Create a display which could be used to advertise the upcoming swimming trials.

Your display should be no more than two metres square in size and should include all the practical information concerning the event. It should be designed to attract people's attention. In addition, the display should have clear branding (in terms of colour, logo and design) running throughout.

The brief indicates a number of things which must be included if students are to complete the task successfully. However, these are left open for students to follow-up as they see fit. The brief has been constructed so as to direct students but not constrain them. The emphasis is on a structure in which students are able to make their own choices and take advantage of their own strengths.

Design briefs need not be constrained to design-led subjects. Here is an example based on a Geography lesson:

Design Brief: Create a presentation which evaluates the United Kingdom's present energy mix.

Your presentation should look at the different elements of the energy mix and should consider the strengths and weaknesses of the overall combination. You should include an interactive element, a drama element and a hand-out. In addition, you should reach a final judgement about the present state of the United Kingdom's energy mix.

Again, the emphasis is on providing a structure but not over-specifying. Students are directed as to what is expected, but it is left up to them how they go about meeting the criteria.

How does it differentiate?

- The activity's openness gives students the opportunity to decide how they will go about completing it. This means that students can engage with the task in way which is suited to their ability levels.
- The activity's structure prevents ambiguity and vagueness. This means that, while students are able to access the task at their own level, this is achieved without recourse to ambiguity or vagueness (which would lead to problems of its own).
- Students can use the separate things specified in the brief to structure their work. This allows them to create their own staging posts and ensures they do not get lost in what might seem at first glance to be a lengthy or complex task.

13. Worksheets

What does it involve?

Here are five ways you can use worksheets to differentiate:

- Create a variety of worksheets in advance of the lesson. These should be aimed at different groups of students in your class and should be categorised according to difficulty level. You could use a model to underpin the variety of sheets, for example: from concrete to abstract.

- Create a number of worksheets which lead on from one another. Students have to work through these. When they complete the first, they move on the second. When they complete the second, they move on to the third. And so on.

- Create a range of worksheets which gradually increase in difficulty. Students then work their way through these, getting as far as they can.

- Create worksheets which include open questions or tasks. These will give students plenty of routes by which to go about completing the work. This, in turn, means that students can opt for a path which plays to their strengths

- Create worksheets which provide students with various options or choices. The reasoning here is the same as was outline din the 'Options' and 'Choices' entries.

How does it differentiate?

- In the first three cases, the variety of worksheets provides students with a variety of options. More able students will be able to work through a number of worksheets, or those which are the most difficult. Less able students will be able to experience success by working through some worksheets or by focussing on ones which are simpler or which contain more concrete (and less abstract) tasks.
- In the last two cases, the worksheets will provide students with a starting-off point (and perhaps some additional structure) which can be dealt with in a way which suits the knowledge and understanding of the student.
- In the third case, the worksheets are akin to a staircase. Through the gradual increase in difficulty, all students will be able to make progress (though most likely at different rates) as they build on that which they have already done.

14. Student Presentations

What does it involve?

Students are divided into groups. Each group is given a topic or question to research. They must then create a presentation for the rest of the class about their particular area. The activity works best when there are a number of disparate topics or questions which all share a connection to the general area of study. It is advisable to set students some success criteria for their presentations. This will provide a structure in which they can work and will help to raise the overall standard of the presentations (by giving the class as a whole something toward which they are aiming).

Here is an example demonstrating the various points just made:

Topic: Sociological perspectives on crime

Task: Groups will be given one of the following perspectives to research:

> Marxism; Functionalism; Feminism; Postmodernism; New Right

> Each group must research their perspective and then create a presentation. This should meet the following success criteria: no reading from slides; an interactive element; appropriate visuals; analysis of how the perspective explains crime; an evaluation of the perspective.

You will note that, in this case, the success criteria are quite specific. They will not always need to be so. It is for the teacher to decide what level of specificity is appropriate. Consideration ought to be given to the needs and ability levels of the students being taught, to the nature of the topic, and to what the teacher is hoping the class will get out of the activity.

How does it differentiate?

- Students are given the opportunity to engage with material at their own speed. While there is a time limit on the creation of the presentations, this is not as severe as it would be if the various items were being looked at one-by-one in a traditional teacher-led setting.
- Students are able to engage with the material on their own terms. Each group has an area to look at and some success criteria to meet, but beyond this it is up to them what approach they take.
- Students learn from one another during the giving of the presentations. This differentiates for two reasons. First, it makes the work accessible in a way that is difficult for the teacher to achieve (because of the social codes the students share and their peer – rather than student-teacher – relationships). Second, the students are presenting the material from their own perspective, which is likely to be different from that of the teacher (and will also probably be shared by their peers).

15. Case Studies

What does it involve?

Case studies provide students with concrete examples of that which they are studying. They contextualise abstract ideas and provide a tangible demonstration of concepts in action. Many things can form the basis of a case study, for example: a person; a group; an event; a decision; an organisation. Two things remain common throughout. First, a single focus is retained. Second, that which forms the basis of the case study offers scope for analysis.

Here are five examples of case studies:

- A person: While studying pacifism in Religious Studies, students could look at Gandhi as a case study. This would contextualise pacifism and associated concepts through the context of Gandhi's life, actions and beliefs.

- A group: While studying the sociology of youth subcultures, students could look at the group of Marxist sociologists who worked at the Centre for Contemporary Cultural Studies (CCCS). This would contextualise many of the key concepts which are used throughout the topic area.

- An event: While studying the history of William Gladstone's various periods as Prime Minister, students could look at his election campaign centred on the 'Bulgarian Horrors'. This would serve to highlight some of the key aspects of Gladstone's thought, character and political attributes.

- A decision: While studying renewable energy, students could look at the decision made by the government over whether or not to invest financially in the development of wind and wave technology. This would serve as a paradigm case through which to consider the arguments for and against renewable energy.

- An organisation: While studying how to change your local community in Citizenship, students could look at a local charity as a case study. This would provide a real-world example of how people have achieved what it is that students are thinking about in their lessons.

How does it differentiate?

- Case studies offer a concrete experience of abstract ideas. They bring concepts to life, making them more accessible to students.
- Students are given the opportunity of looking at something small (the case study) in order to understand something big (the concepts and ideas). This provides a simple, accessible means by which all pupils can come to terms with notions that are complex or challenging.
- If the case study focuses on a person, or if that which it consists of has a human element, then this gives students something to which they can relate. In turn, this makes the work more accessible – pupils have the kind of purchase which might not be attainable through a more abstract approach.

16. Discovery Learning

What does it involve?

In discovery learning, students are encouraged to discover facts and relationships themselves. The teacher facilitates the learning so as to create situations in which students might discover things and work things out. It is expected that students will follow their own paths given a starting point the teacher has provided. As a result, it cannot be guaranteed that particular learning will take place. With that said, the concomitant fact is that the learning which does take place will be led by the student and is likely to concern paths of thinking in which they are interested and by which they are motivated.

Discovery learning can take many forms. It could be highly circumscribed or left open. It could be manifested as a discrete activity or as a single element within some other type of activity. It could be something which a teacher calls on from time-to-time, or an approach which is used to underpin all that a teacher does. Here are some examples of how and when discovery learning might be used:

- Group work. For example, students are given a question which they must explore while working in groups. They will come to 'discover' an answer to this question based on their joint explorations.

- Providing some of the information and letting students work out the rest. For example, students might be given some background information concerning the years preceding the Great Crash. They would then be left to infer what might have happened before investigating the facts in order to discover what actually turned out to be the case.

- Setting students independent tasks such as research or a design brief. The rationale here is that students are being taken in a certain direction and then left to make their own way (within the guidelines provided).

- Experiments. Experimenting is, by it is very nature, an act intimately tied up with discovery. Experiments need not be confined to science lessons; they can be brought into other subjects through the use of a testing procedure (students develop a hypothesis and then test to see whether it holds or not), although this might require some minor adaptations.

- Investigations. These are similar to experiments. Again, the nature of the act is such that it is closely tied up with discovery. If one is investigating something, it is inevitable that discoveries are being sought.

How does it differentiate?

- Students are given the opportunity to direct their own learning. This makes the task more accessible as it is led by the learner rather than being at the behest of the teacher.
- There is clear purpose to what students are doing, and this purpose (discovery) is tied up with human instincts concerning curiosity and the desire to know. The sense of purpose

enhances motivation – students see that they have an achievable and meaningful goal towards which their actions are being directed.

- Knowledge is being presented as provisional rather than fixed. Pupils are being encouraged to find things out for themselves, rather than to ingest (or reject) that which is given to them by the teacher or some other source (such as a textbook).

17. Task Mixture

What does it involve?

Use a mixture of tasks. This will ensure that your students have a variety of opportunities, each of which will be asking slightly different things of them. By planning in this way, you will be helping to make certain that pupils have the chance to play to their strengths on a number of occasions. In turn, this will make them feel more at ease when faced with tasks which they might find more difficult.

Having a task mixture prevents students from feeling that 'we only do things one way' (and what if that one approach happens to be a way that some students find really difficult to access?). As pointed out above, this brings benefits in terms of learning. It also brings rewards in terms of psychology. Variety creates interest and enhances motivation. For proof of this, one need only recall the tedium associated with a repetitive job.

You can use a mixture of tasks:

- In a single lesson.

- Across a unit of work.

- Across the year as a whole.

You might like to develop a collection of task-types with which you feel comfortable and stick to these. Or, you might like to continue testing out different approaches in order to ascertain what works best for your various classes. Personally, I find that different collections of task-types work well with different age groups. I also like to throw in completely different tasks from time-to-time so as to generate a sense of surprise and excitement.

How does it differentiate?

- A mixture of tasks means that students are being asked to do a range of different things. There is therefore a high likelihood that the teacher will be playing to the strengths of a variety of different students.
- Avoiding repetition results in increased motivation. This, in turn, leads to increased engagement across the board.
- A mixture of tasks means different types of thinking. Pupils will be stretched and challenged to use their minds in a range of ways. This will see them interacting with content and ideas from various perspectives.

18. Task Mixture II

What does it involve?

An alternative way to judge whether you have a mixture of tasks is to look at what you are asking students to produce. This is a little like working backwards.

When planning a lesson or a unit of work, identify a mixture of products you would like students to have created by the end of it. Base your activities on this list and they cannot fail to be a mixture. You will have no choice but to use a range of tasks in order to ensure the various items are produced. Here is a list of some possible products:

- Report
- Poem
- Essay
- Poster
- Advert
- Design
- Speech
- Role-Play
- Summary
- Story
- Comic Strip
- Plan
- Article
- Presentation
- Booklet

One may decide prior to planning a lesson that it would be beneficial for students to have produced a design, an advert and a speech by the end of it. Having settled on these products, a series of activities could be placed in conjunction in order to form the lesson. These tasks would need to be different in order to result in the production of a design, an advert and a speech.

How does it differentiate?

- A range of tasks means that students have various opportunities to access and engage with the work. There is a higher likelihood that all students will find something in the lesson in which they can succeed.
- The creation of different products requires various skills. By having a range of products which you want pupils to create, you will be ensuring that you play to the strengths of a large number of those who are in your class.
- As noted in the previous entry, variety enhances motivation and avoids the disengagement that may occur as a result of repetition.

19. Envoys

What does it involve?

Envoys is a group work task that is especially good for differentiating. It works as follows:

The class is divided into groups. Each group is made up of three or four pupils. Groups are given an area of the topic to investigate. Questions may be assigned in order to provide direction. Each group is given the materials necessary to complete their investigations. A time limit is set.

Upon the calling of time, each group stops what it is doing and elects an envoy. This student stands up and moves to another group. They then teach this group about what they have discovered in the course of their investigations. When this has been done, envoys move off to teach another group. The activity continues until all the groups have been visited by all the envoys.

The teacher can provide a pro-forma to students on which they make notes concerning what they are taught. This means the information is captured. It also provides some further structure to the teachings section of the task.

Here is an example of an envoys task:

A class of twenty-four students is divided into six groups. There are four pupils in each group. The topic is climate change. The following questions are assigned, one to each group:

- What causes climate change?
- What effects has climate change had so far?
- What effects might climate change produce in the future?
- How might climate change be stopped?
- What is renewable energy?
- What is sustainable development

Each group researches their question and then elects an envoy. These students leave their group and teach what has been found out to the rest of the class. By the end of the activity, students have information concerning all six of the questions.

How does it differentiate?

- In terms of group work, the same points apply as are detailed in the 'Group Work' entry.
- Students are able to learn from one another, rather than from the teacher or some other source (such as a video). This makes the information accessible and engaging – students share social codes and perceive their peers differently from how they perceive the teacher.
- The role of 'envoy' is often taken on by more able students. This gives them an opportunity to be stretched and challenged; they will have to carefully consider how to communicate the information their group has discovered so as to ensure it is understood by their peers.

20. Peer Research

What does it involve?

This activity involves students eliciting information from their peers about the topic being studied. It works as follows:

Students are introduced to the topic. The teacher explains that each pupil must create a questionnaire, ten questions in length, which they can use to interview their peers about the subject area. When pupils have come up with their questions, they stand up and walk around the room, interviewing as many people as they can. Students should record their results as they go along.

The teacher should set a time limit for the interviewing section of the activity and should also encourage students to aim for a certain number of interviews (which will be determined by the length of time available, the type of questions which are being asked and the number of students in the class). It is advisable for the teacher to highlight at the beginning of the activity the fact that students will have to record their results and then either write these up or use them as the basis of a discussion. The reason for this is that it compels students to think carefully about the questions they will ask and the likely information these particular questions will elicit. The task is usually most effective when students have a mixture of quantitative (numerical), qualitative (non-numerical), open and closed questions.

Here are five examples of topics which could be used to order peer research:

- Crime. Students studying crime in Citizenship or Sociology could investigate their peers' experience of and feelings about crime.
- Family. Students who are engaged in a piece of work connected to the family could investigate their peers' experience of the family. This could then be compared to whatever they are studying (for example, the family in medieval times).
- Responses to a text or a series of texts. Students could interview one another in order to find out about the various responses people have had to a particular text or series of texts.
- At the end of a unit of work students could interview one another in order to find out what they think about the big questions underpinning the topic.
- At the end of a unit of work students could interview one another in order to find out what they thought about the topic and how they found the various pedagogical methods employed by the teacher.

How does it differentiate?

- Students develop their own questions. This means that they are able to work at their own level and to focus on aspects of the topic which interest them.
- The teacher can model good questions (or use those produced by certain students as a model). This helps all students in the class to access the work.
- Pupils are in charge of their own learning and thus are more likely to be motivated (and they are more likely to see meaning and purpose in what they are doing). They are developing their own questions, they are choosing who to interview and they are writing up their own results.

21. Activity Stations

What does it involve?

The task works as follows:

- Set up a number of different stations around the room.

- Each station should have a different resource and/or task attached to it.

- Ensure that there are a variety of types of resource and task. For example: you might have a case study, a laptop with a video on it, a card sort, a hand-out, a diamond nine and a newspaper article.

- Put students in groups and assign each group to a station.

- Rotate the groups after a set length of time. Aim for each group to visit each station.

The purpose of the activity is to provide students with a variety of different ways by which to engage with a topic. Their journey around the activity stations might be supplemented by a pro-forma which is to be filled in at each point, by a set of overarching questions which are to order pupils' thinking at each station, or it might be left open and followed-up through a discussion focussing on that which students found to be of most interest.

How does it differentiate?

- By providing a range of different resources or tasks at each activity station, the teacher will be ensuring that pupils interact with the lesson content in a variety of different ways. This will lead to an increase in motivation, maintenance of engagement and a higher chance that all students will find something that plays to their strengths.
- The range of resources and tasks will challenge students to think about the topic in a number of different ways. This is likely to result in all pupils being stretched, regardless of the point at which they start.
- Each activity station provides a different route into the topic. This means that students will have multiple opportunities to get to grips with the key concepts and ideas. In addition, each time students move stations, they will be challenged to reassess that which they have learnt about the topic so far. This will stretch their thinking.

22. Visits and Visitors

What does it involve?

Visits and visitors are a great way of differentiating. They are engaging for students for the following reasons:

- They are interactive.

- They are unusual.

- They are a change to the routine.

- They bring learning alive.

- They are different to most of what goes on in the classroom.

It is a good idea to plan work around a visit or visitor so that students get as much as possible from the experience. It will also help to ensure their learning is captured in order that it might be built on and used in subsequent lessons. Here are five things you might plan around visits or visitors:

i. If you have a visitor coming in to your lesson, work with your students to create a set of questions that you will ask them.

ii. If you have a visitor coming in to your lesson, divide your class into groups and ask each group to research a different aspect of the topic which the visitor is to talk about. This could be developed by instructing the groups to create a short presentation which could be given to the rest of the class and the visitor.

iii. If you are going on a visit, spend time beforehand working with your students to explore ideas, people, events and concepts connected to the place you are to visit.

iv. Provide students with a worksheet which they have to fill in during the course of their visit. This could be structured so as to feel like an investigation.

v. In either case, follow-up the experience by asking students to create something encompassing all that happened (or focussing on a specific aspect). For example, pupils could write a newspaper report, create a poster or design a website about their visit or about the visitor who came into school.

How does it differentiate?

- Visits and visitors are a change to the routine. As such, they offer students the chance to experience something different and to step out of normal habits. For these reasons they are likely to be engaging and motivational.

- Visits and visitors are interactive. In the first case, students are going out into the world and learning in context. In the second case, students have the opportunity to talk and interact with someone who comes from outside of school and has an area of expertise which is unlikely to be replicated in the teaching staff.

- In both cases, the normal 'rules' of school life are temporarily suspended. By this I do not mean the rules concerning behaviour, good manners and the like. Rather, I mean the tacit rules governing how students and teachers interact, the nature of classroom learning and the expectations of what will happen during the course of a lesson. The upending of these 'rules' creates a space in which students can act differently and in which learning can take place in unfamiliar ways.

23. Drama

What does it involve?

Drama is a broad category within which many activity types are subsumed. Here are five which can be used in nearly any lesson:

- Creation of a role-play. This involves students being given some material which they must demonstrate or showcase through a role-play. For example, in a Citizenship lesson concerning consumer rights, one group may be asked to role-play the Food Safety Act. This would involve them creating a short piece demonstrating what the act entailed as well as how, when and where it might be applied.

- Role-playing of something which already exists. This involves students being given a text which they turn into a role-play. For example, in an English lesson the class might be divided into pairs, with each pair being given an extract from Macbeth. Students would then have to read out and dramatize the extract, with various performances subsequently shown to the whole class.

- Freeze-frame. Students are put into groups. A topic, concept or statement is provided for the whole class, or a number of different ones are assigned, one to each group. Pupils are expected to create a freeze-frame depicting or related to that which they have been asked to consider. A freeze-frame is a point at which the action has been stopped. There is a before and an after, but this remains unknown to the audience (it is for them to infer, based on what they see before them). Students create their freeze-frames and then show them to the rest of the class. Discussion ensues.

- Mime or charades. Students are divided into teams. Members of each team take it in turns to mime a concept, key word or idea connected to the topic of study. The rest of the team try to correctly guess what it is that is being mimed.

- Modelling. Students are asked to use their bodies to create a model of a concept, key word or idea. One way to structure this is to have half the class displaying their models while the other half walk around and examine them. The two halves then swap over.

How does it differentiate?

- Drama requires a different approach and different ways of thinking from many other modes of learning. Using it as part of lessons gives students the opportunity to engage with the work in a way which is likely to be quite different from that which is seen as the norm.
- Tasks based on drama are often fun and create the opportunity for students to move beyond the traditional formalities of classroom learning (such as being seated, working at desks and remaining quiet for much of the lesson). They are likely to engage students as a result.
- In all the activities outlined above, students are expected to synthesise information. This is so that they can recreate it in dramatic form. Synthesis is challenging – particularly if it is to be done well. Drama tasks therefore stretch and challenge students in terms of their thinking.

24. Extension Tasks

What does it involve?

An extension task is something which is added on to a segment of a lesson in order to stretch the thinking of students who complete the main activity. It can take many forms but ought always to involve a greater degree of complexity or challenge than that which has gone before it. Extension tasks are not confined to the most able students; they are for all students who complete the main activity. Pupils will engage with them on their own terms (for example, more able students may produce more nuanced responses) but may require some assistance to get going. Here are five examples of extension tasks which could be used in a wide range of lessons:

- A philosophically-informed or concept-led question relating to that which is being studied. This will require students to think more deeply about the topic and the ideas upon which it rests.
- A question which asks students to evaluate or synthesise information relating to the topic. Both these skills require high-order, abstract thinking. Questions based on such processes will therefore cause students to think more deeply about the information at issue.
- A task which must be completed in a short amount of time (that being precisely specified). Given a certain window in which to act, one must think quickly and carefully. Decisions have to be made at speed and attention must be given to the work itself as well as the time-scale in which the work is being completed. Such a task is challenging as a result.
- Students are asked to write and answer an exam-style question about the area of study. The challenge here is two-fold. First, pupils are compelled to think about the topic from the outside; this stands in contrast to what they are likely to have done previously in the lesson. Second, they have to manipulate that which they have learnt so as to create an appropriate response to the question they have written.
- Students are asked to rewrite their work so that it is shorter and clearer while still retaining the same meaning. The challenge stems from students having to synthesise their own work such that it communicates more accurately that which they first intended.

How does it differentiate?

- Extension tasks are a way to stretch and challenge students who work more swiftly than the majority of the class.
- They encourage those students who quickly get to grips with an activity or topic to think more deeply about that which is being studied.

- They cause students to reassess that which they have already done in a lesson and to think about it with greater care. In a sense, extension tasks re-contextualise that which has gone before.

25. Further Reading

What does it involve?

A way in which to challenge students who complete the work you have set before the rest of the class have finished is to give them further reading. This could come in a number of forms:

- Newspaper, magazine or website articles connected to your subject.
- Extracts from books connected to the topic or subject.
- Textbooks containing information beyond that which has been looked at in class.
- Textbook extracts in which the material studied in class is considered at a more sophisticated level. For example, this might involve GCSE students been given an extract from an A Level textbook.
- An essay written by a student higher up the school concerning the topic being studied.

In the first and last case, the teacher can put together and laminate a collection of these items. This means that they are readily to hand and can be used again and again.

Further reading is of benefit to students as an end in itself. With that said, here are five ways in which you can structure the reading should you so wish:

i.   Provide students with a set of questions which they are to answer once they have completed the reading. This is a comprehension exercise.

ii. Provide students with one question or statement which is to inform their reading or which they are to respond to having done the reading. For example: How might the ideas put forward by the author connect to what we have studied today?

iii. Ask students to summarise the reading. This could be caveated by a further instruction such as: 'in no more than three sentences,' or 'for an audience of young children.'

iv. Give students time to complete the reading. When they have done so, engage them in a discussion about the text. This could centre on understanding of what has been written, the relative merits of the piece, or an analysis of how it connects to the lesson.

v.   Ask students to translate the text. By this I do not mean from one language to another, but instead from written English into a diagram, comic strip, flow chart or some other such visual means of communication.

How does it differentiate?

- Students who have completed the work are given an opportunity to explore the topic or the subject in greater depth.
- The teacher can select reading material which will challenge students' thinking.
- Through the use of the structuring activities outlined above, the teacher can encourage students to think in different ways about the topic. It is likely that, because of the texts being considered, these will necessarily be more complex and challenging than that which has formed the basis of the main activities.

Chapter Three – Questioning

In this chapter we look at fifteen activities, strategies and techniques connected to questioning. You can use all of them to differentiate your lessons.

1. Wonder Wall

What does it involve?

This technique was first introduced to me by my friend and fellow teacher, James Wright. My interpretation of it is as follows:

Create a space on your classroom wall called the 'Wonder Wall'. You might like to make this look like a wall by chalking a brick pattern onto black paper. When students think of questions and there is not enough time to explore these, ask them to write them on a Post-It® note and to stick this onto the 'Wonder Wall.' Here are three ways in which you might go on to utilise these questions in your lesson:

- When students have finished a task in which the rest of the class is still engaged, invite them to go up to the 'Wonder Wall' and to select a question from it. They should then answer this question either in writing or through a discussion with another student who has finished the main activity.

- When enough questions have been added to the 'Wonder Wall', plan a lesson, or lesson segment, in which these are distributed around the class to pairs or groups, who then discuss them. When this has been done, groups either team up and share answers with one another, or envoys leave their original groups in order to share answers with the rest of the class.

- Build some time into lessons during which you invite one or more students to select a question from the 'Wonder Wall' which you then discuss with them. This could be used as a reward or as a means of creating interactions with specific students.

How does it differentiate?

- In the first case, the students who take the questions from the 'Wonder Wall' are being challenged to think further and to produce work which is over and above that which the rest of the class is doing. You might like to actively encourage students to think of big, difficult or unusual questions to put on the wall.
- In the second case, students have created the questions about which the activity is structured. This encourages engagement and gives a sense of ownership. In addition, by using discussion and encouraging the sharing of answers, all students will have an opportunity to be involved in the activity and to learn from one another.
- In the third case, the teacher is able to provide tailored support to the students with whom they have a discussion. They will be able to pitch their questions and comments at an appropriate level and provide the right level of challenge and scaffolding.

2. Individual Questioning

What does it involve?

The teacher asks questions to individual students. This could be one-on-one, during group activities, or as part of a whole-class discussion. It is expected that the teacher will plan in advance who they will question and why, though this need only involve a momentary assessment of the options available.

Individual questioning is of great benefit for two reasons. First, it allows the teacher to tailor their questions to the particular student in question. Over time, the teacher will build up a picture of each of their students in terms of where they are at, where their strengths lie and in what areas they need help making progress. All this can be called upon when asking questions of individuals. Here is an example of how questioning may differ depending on the student:

Topic: The use of imagery in poetry writing

Question to Student A, who has shown that they are highly-skilled at English: How might poets seek to control that which readers see in their minds?

Question to Student B, who finds English more difficult: What images might you use to make a reader think of sadness?

You will note that the difference here is one of degree. In the first case, the question is essentially an abstract matter – it asks the student to deal with generalities. In the second case, the question is more concrete. It asks the student to think about a specific example of the use of images.

The second benefit inherent in individual questioning is that it results in students having time in which to talk with the teacher. This means the teacher can elicit information from them and is able to assess where they are at. It also allows the student the opportunity to make progress in their thinking through articulating their ideas to someone who is in a position to develop them, build on them and challenge them (or, if necessary, tease them out).

How does it differentiate?

- Individual questioning involves the teacher pitching questions to specific students. Therefore, the teacher will be tailoring their questions to the needs and ability levels of those students.
- The teacher can use individual questioning to target specific students in the class. This could be in parallel to the main activity, or it could supplement the activity. In either case, the

teacher is able to challenge and stretch the thinking of more able students or support and scaffold that of less able pupils.

- Students who are questioned are given specific time by the teacher. They will be aware of this and will be likely to respond as a result (appreciating that they are, for a short period at least, the sole focus of the teacher's attention).

3. Questioning that Promotes Reasoning

What does it involve?

Reasoning is the skill that underpins most of what goes on in school. Its importance cannot be underestimated. A student who can reason adroitly is likely to do well across the board. A student who struggles to reason is likely to find much of the curriculum difficult to access. Questions which promote reasoning are therefore good for all students. They encourage pupils to think in a rational way and to articulate this thinking to their peers.

When posing questions to students, consider whether the question you are asking promotes reasoning. If it does not, ask yourself whether you can alter it so that it does. Here are some examples of questions which promote reasoning:

- Why might X be the case?
- For what reasons might X be true?
- How might X have turned out as it did?
- What reasons do you have to support what you have just said?
- How might someone argue against the answer we have just heard?

In each case, pupils are called on to reason. They are asked to consider something in the light of reason and to articulate an answer which is predicated on a rational way of thinking.

It will undoubtedly be the case that in any one class you will have students who respond to such questions with varying levels of sophistication. What ought to be common all the responses though, is the presence of reasoning. By asking questions which promote this, you will be helping all your pupils to develop their rational mind – regardless of where they begin from or how adept they presently are at reasoning.

A good model to use for this type of questioning is as follows:

- Ask students the question and tell them to think about this on their own.
- When a little time has passed, invite pupils to get into pairs and to explain their answers to one another.
- Move around the classroom, listening in to students' conversations. Step in if necessary or appropriate.
- Bring the class back together and get a number of students to share their answers.
- Scrutinise these answers as a class (calling on reason to do so). If appropriate, explain to students what is the correct answer (in many cases this will not be necessary).

How does it differentiate?

- Questions that promote reasoning engage all students. This is because all students possess the capacity – to various degrees – to reason.
- They also challenge all students by asking them to think logically and rationally about the subject of the classroom.
- Through using the model, you will expose students to a range of reasoned thinking. This will help them to identify and absorb good practice from their peers.

4. Serial Questioning

What does it involve?

Serial questioning means asking a series of questions. This may be done:

- In direct conversation with a student, group or the whole-class.
- As a segment of a lesson.
- As an overarching framework for a whole lesson.

Serial questioning has two major advantages in terms of differentiation.

First, it allows the teacher to challenge students by asking a series of questions which gradually develop in difficulty. By taking such an approach, the teacher is likely to keep most (or all) of the class engaged while encouraging them to think in ways which are progressively more complex. An example of this would be during a segment of a lesson when the teacher sets students a collection of questions to answer. Each one requires a written response which is a little more complicated than that which came previous. Pupil progress is therefore scaffolded – each question takes students a little bit higher, helping them to access that which comes next.

Second, it allows the teacher to actively respond to the answers students give. This is only possible if the teacher is asking a series of questions in conversation. It is not possible if the questions are written down. An example would be if the teacher was in conversation with a student who was struggling to come to terms with the work. Through using a series of questions, the teacher could lead the student from what they do know to what they need to know in order to be successful in the lesson. The teacher's questions would be shaped by the information provided by the student at each stage. It is an interactive process, one which is led by the teacher's developing understanding of where the student is at and how the gap to where they need to be might be closed.

How does it differentiate?

- Serial questioning offers the opportunity to challenge the thinking of the whole class through a gradual increase in the difficulty level of the questions being asked.
- When serial questioning is used in conversation, it provides the teacher with the chance to respond to what students say. This means they can shape the questions they ask to suit the needs of the student.
- Through using serial questioning in conversation, the teacher is in a position to help students to bridge the gap between what they know and what they need to know, regardless of the position in which they start.

5. Challenging Questions

What does it involve?

Challenging questions are those which push students to think differently about a topic. They may be harder than normal questions, more profound, more complex, more unusual, more esoteric or more creative. In fact, challenging questions can take on a whole range of different forms. The key thing, which remains common throughout, is that for a question to be challenging it ought to stray beyond the normal or standard type of thinking which goes on in the classroom. Here are some examples of challenging questions, replete with explanations of why they are challenging:

- What is 56732 x 281? This question is hard. It involves more difficult calculations than (we assume) have been required in the main activity. Such a question takes the core premise of the main activity – in this case multiplication of large numbers – and enhances the degree of difficulty associated with it.

- What does it mean to 'do wrong'? This question is profound. It asks students to consider a concept which has been used during the lesson, but which has not been interrogated directly. In this sense, the question is also philosophical; it asks students to analyse that whish they use to think (concepts and categories).

- If we take 'good' to mean that which society seeks to promote, and we assume that individuals in society will gain benefits from doing what it wishes, why then do people still commit crimes? This question is complex. The effect has been achieved through the use of qualifying clauses. The question is modified by the use of these. Students must take these into account when they are answering. Therefore, there is more for them to think about.

- How might life be different if graphs did not exist? This question is unusual. It takes an aspect of the lesson (in this case graphs) and asks students to think about it in a way which is quite alien to that which will have been required by the main activities. Through this, students' understanding of the aspect is likely to develop.

- How might a different outcome have been possible in the War of the Roses? This question is creative. It is asking students to think imaginatively about the topic. Through doing this, students will be caused to look at that which they have been studying from different angles and perspectives.

How does it differentiate?

- Challenging questions cause students to think in a variety of different ways.
- Challenging questions stretch students. They help them to think about ideas and information in ways which are different to the standard approaches to knowledge taken in the classroom.

- A variety of students can engage with challenging questions. The level at which they do this will likely be determined by their prior knowledge and understanding; they will find the point which is right for them.

6. Open and Closed

What does it involve?

Open and closed questions have different structures. Here are some examples:

1.1 How old are you?

1.2 What do you think – yes or no?

1.3 Did it happen on Monday?

2.1 What does youth feel like?

2.2 What are your thoughts?

2.3 When might it have happened?

In each of the cases 1.1, 1.2 and 1.3, the question is formed so as to demand a specific response. The respondent has only a few options available (and these have been stated or implied by the questioner); they are expected to provide a short answer – a little piece of information.

In the cases 2.1, 2.2 and 2.3, the questions have been left open. They are not circumscribed and, in fact, invite the respondent to give a lengthy, detailed answer – one in which they are exploring the contents of their mind.

It is the nature of closed questions that they generate severely limited and highly specific information. In some situations this is useful. For example, on a form one has to fill in at the Post Office. In other situations this becomes a serious limitation. For example, in the classroom when one is trying to help students to learn.

Asking a higher proportion of open questions is good for differentiation. It means that the teacher can assess more clearly what students think and why – and then use this information to modify their teaching. In addition, it gives pupils the opportunity to share their thoughts and ideas about a topic. This is in contrast to closed questioning which – generally – is used to request specific answers. Open questioning diminishes the stakes. Students are less likely to feel they are in a game where they can lose (by not giving the correct answer) and feel embarrassed. They are therefore more likely to engage with the lesson. If open questioning is used consistently over time, students will come to see that learning in the classroom is a collaborative process in which all can take part and in which all are made to feel at ease.

How does it differentiate?

- Open questions help the teacher to gain more information about what students think. They can use this to adapt their teaching to the needs of their students.
- Open questions diminish the stakes. They make it less likely that students will perceive questioning as a failure/success exercise and more as a collaborative learning experience.
- Open questions are more accessible than closed questions. They do not rely on students having a certain, specific piece of information. Instead, they allow all students to share what they think.

7. Clarification

What does it involve?

Clarification questions include examples such as:

What do you mean by that?

Could you explain that in another way?

Is there an example you could use to show what you mean?

These types of questions are concerned with helping the respondent to make their ideas clearer and easier to understand. They do this in two ways. First, they elicit more information from the speaker. Second, they cause the speaker to consider what it is they have said, what it is they are trying to convey, and the relationship between these two things.

Clarification questions are thus two-part in nature. They serve to draw more from the person being questioned and they cause that person to think again about their ideas.

We can see from this why it is appropriate for the teacher to use such questions. Regardless of where the students is at in terms of knowledge or understanding, asking clarifying questions will help them to develop, simplify and refine their ideas. In this sense, the act is one which is, by its very nature, differentiate. It matters not where the student is at, by asking clarifying questions the teacher will be helping them to advance their thinking.

How does it differentiate?

- Clarifying questions cause all students, regardless of their starting position, to develop and refine their ideas.

- They also cause all students to communicate their ideas more clearly. This results in the teacher and student having a better notion of what is being talked about and why.
- By using clarifying questions, the teacher elicits more information. They thus have a better understanding of where their students are at, what they are thinking and how they are thinking. This makes it easier for the teacher to adapt their teaching to meet the needs of their students.

8. Question Planning

What does it involve?

Very simply, this involves the teacher planning their questions prior to the lesson. Here are three ways in which you might think about your question planning:

- Are there any students of whom I particularly want to ask questions? If so, what questions will I ask them?

    It might be that you have identified a student who is very able and that you want to develop some challenging questions to ask them. Alternatively, you might have noted that two students seem to be having a great deal of difficulty with the work and would benefit from some supportive questioning. A third possibility could be that you have a student who is quiet. In this case, some targeted questioning would help you to elicit information from them regarding where they are at and how they are finding the topic.

- Are there any particular types of question that I would like to ask? If so, what are they?

    It might be that you want to push the thinking of the whole class by getting them to evaluate some of the ideas with which you have been working. Alternatively, you might want to encourage greater reflection and therefore plan some appropriate questions. Finally, it may be that you feel not enough independent learning has been taking place and that some creative questions could help rectify the situation.

- What information would you like to elicit from the students in your class? What questions will help you to draw this out?

  In order to ensure your teaching is meeting the needs of your students, you might like to focus on eliciting certain information from them (with this then informing what you do). Planning questions in advance will help you to ensure you draw out the information you require.

How does it differentiate?

- Planning questions in advance allows you to target specific students. Therefore, you can challenge and support those students who are more and less able.
- Planning questions in advance means that you can focus on eliciting certain information from your students. In turn, this makes it easier for you to adapt your teaching to meet their needs.
- Planning questions in advance means that you do not have to think them up during the lesson. This means, in turn, that you are better placed to observe and interact with your students. The result will be teaching which is more agile and finely-tuned.

9. Question Range

What does it involve?

Mountain ranges are made up of a collection of different peaks. All of these will have many things in common – this is what causes them to be classified together – but they also retain individual differences. It may be that one of the peaks is particularly tall, that another is largely inaccessible, that a third is frequented by day-trippers and that a fourth is blanketed with thick gorse.

A question range is, in principle, the same as a mountain range. It contains a number of items which are in large part alike – sufficiently so to be classified as belonging to the same category – but which also retain (sometimes significant) individual differences.

Let us imagine that a mountain-climbing club has organised a trip to a mountain range. Upon arrival, the group splits in three – the separate assemblies being based on experience and ability. One group sets off to tackle the most taxing climb, another ventures onto an intermediate route, and the third chooses the easiest option. At the end of the day all the mountaineers meet up. They swap stories. It is clear that they each understand that to which the other is referring and that all of them have had a challenging day. They have two things in common: the experience of climbing a mountain and the experience of having been tested.

The same principle applies during a lesson when a teacher makes use of a question range. This involves them having a selection of questions which possess varying levels of difficulty. They ask some questions to the whole class, some to certain groups and some to specific students. Here are five ways in which you might go about forming a question range:

- Use the two poles of concrete and abstract. Ask a variety of questions along the continuum which forms in between these opposite ends. Concrete questions deal with facts, examples and specifics. Abstract questions deal with ideas, concepts and generalities.
- Use Bloom's Taxonomy. This provides a hierarchy of categories you can use as the basis of questions (knowledge, comprehension, application, analysis, synthesis, evaluation).

- Use language that varies in its sophistication. You might ask questions of a number of students that, in terms of meaning, are ostensibly the same but which in terms of phrasing are qualitatively different.
- Use questions that run from simple to complex. The varying degree of difficulty might be due to the sentence formation you use, that which the questions are about, or the extent of technical vocabulary on which you call.
- Use questions which vary in their proximity to the subject. You might have some questions which are focussed on the central issues of the topic and others which are tangentially related.

How does it differentiate?

- A range of questions means a range of levels. This in turn means different students in the class can engage with different questions that you ask.
- Having a range of questions available allows the teacher to pick out that which is most appropriate, depending on to whom they are talking.
- By having a range of questions, you are more likely to take account of the varying levels of understanding your pupils possess.

10. Justify

What does it involve?

Justification is the providing of support to a claim. In the strongest sense – and this is the one we want to promote with our students – it will involve the provision of reasons, evidence and examples. We will look briefly at why each of these can be said to give justification for a statement.

Reasons provide an explanation for why something is said to be the case. Different reasons may appeal to different things for their explanatory power. This may include logic, 'fit', prior knowledge, correlation and so on. Not all reasons are equally valid. Nor are all appeals made by reasons equally sound.

Evidence provides an empirical reference point for that which has been stated. It points to something in the world and indicates that this is support for the claim. It represents a drawing together of the abstract and the concrete. The latter – the evidence – is said to prove, or to go some way to proving, the former to be the case.

Examples provide specificity. They demonstrate a particular case of a general statement. By using an example, one makes that which is abstract clearer and easier to understand. In addition, examples tie the abstract or general statement to the real world. This process offers support to the claim being made because it indicates how the claim manifests itself empirically.

By asking students to justify the claims they make, the teacher is encouraging them to use reasons, evidence and examples. Therefore, they are encouraging them to think better and to create stronger arguments. Examples of questions which provoke justification include:

Why might that be true?

What evidence do you have for that?

How might you convince someone what you have said is actually the case?

Such questions differentiate because they cause all students, regardless of their starting position, to think about how they might construct a means of support for that which they are claiming to be the case. A very able student might be in a position to create a sophisticated justification; a less able student might come up with an argument which is not quite as persuasive. Common to both however, will be a sustained attempt to justify what it is they have claimed to be the case.

How does it differentiate?

- Questions which ask for justification can be asked of all students, regardless of their starting position.
- Such questions cause all students to think rationally about what they have said and to look for reasons, evidence and examples which might provide support.
- All students will make progress from their starting position through being encouraged to justify their claims.

11. Students Ask Questions

What does it involve?

Getting students to ask questions is a great way to differentiate. Here are five ways in which you might make it happen:

- Invite one or two students to lead the class in a discussion. You might like to choose students who are particularly able or who are confident speakers and performers. These pupils take on the teacher's role, asking questions of the whole-class, of groups and of individuals. They manage the discussion and help the class to develop their ideas together.
- Give every student in the class a slip of paper. Ask them to write on this a question they would like answered – or which they would like to ask to the class. Collect the completed pieces of paper in and shuffle them. Invite a student to pick out a question at random. The class then discuss this question.
- Give every student a slip of paper. Ask them to write on this a question they would like answered in the next lesson or which

they would like the class to discuss. Collect these from students as they leave the classroom. Look at them before the next lesson and select some to pursue. At the start of the next lesson, ask the students whose questions have been selected to explain why they wrote them.

- Invite students to ask you questions about the topic. If any arise that you cannot answer, explain that you and the class will endeavour to investigate these further.

- Put students in groups of four. Designate one member of each group 'the questioner'. These students team up and develop a set of questions related to the topic. They then use these questions to stimulate discussion among their group members.

How does it differentiate?

- Encouraging students to ask questions involves them in the lesson and causes them to think actively about the topic in hand. This makes lessons engaging and gives students a sense of ownership over their learning.

- Students will be able to engage with the topic at their own level by asking questions based on their own thinking. This means that all students can interact with the ideas and information being studied, regardless of their starting point.

- By having students ask questions, the teacher is taking a step back and inviting their pupils to play a bigger role in the learning. This encourages them to be independent and to direct the lesson toward areas in which they are interested. This is motivational and enhances learner engagement.

12. Thinking Time

What does it involve?

It can be so tempting to ask a question in expectation of an immediate response. Sometimes it feels as if there is an in-built reflex which causes one to demand an answer barely a second after the upward inflection has floated forward into the air. Reasons for this might include a desire for pace, a fear of silence, the learned experience we all have from our own schooling, countless hours of television detective and courtroom dramas or something else entirely. Whatever it is that has led to this position does not matter too much. What matters is that we try to avoid it happening.

We can do this by giving thinking time. This involves the teacher asking a question and then waiting. During the intervening period, they ask students to think about the question. Only when sufficient time has passed (perhaps twenty or thirty seconds) does the teacher seek to elicit responses from their pupils.

The result is that all members of the class have an opportunity to process what has been said and, in turn, to formulate an answer. Two major benefits flow from this. First, the overall standard of the responses is likely to be higher. This is because all students will have been able to think about what answer they might give. Second, all students will be able to engage with the question. This is because the thinking time provides a space in which less able students can consider and reflect upon the question and what it means.

Here are five ways in which you might indicate to pupils that you are giving them thinking time:

- 'OK, thirty seconds silent thinking about the question.'
- 'What are your thoughts on this? Have a think to yourself and then we'll hear some responses.'

- 'Have a look at this question (which is displayed on the board). I'm going to leave it up there and let you think about it before we start our discussion.'
- 'Why do cats have fur? I'd like you to think about this for a few moments. When I indicate, I'd like to you to share your thoughts with your partner.
- 'How might tomorrow be different from today? Take a few moments to think about the question. When you are ready, note down your thoughts.'

How does it differentiate?

- All students are given the opportunity to think carefully about the question. This means that all students can engage with the question – it stops those students who are particularly able from dominating, but it also avoids feelings of failure when less able students find it difficult to answer immediately.
- Students who swiftly come to answers are encouraged to think at length. This may be in contrast to their normal way of doing things. The result is that they will be challenged to reflect on and develop their first thoughts.
- The teacher can use the thinking time to talk to individual students or to observe the class and assess their body language. Both of these possibilities will allow the teacher to elicit information about how students are dealing with the question.

13. Rephrasing Questions

What does it involve?

To rephrase something is to put it differently – to use an alternative set of words in order to communicate a similar meaning. Here are three ways in which you might rephrase questions while teaching:

- Ask a question using the terminology which is appropriate for the subject. Repeat the question using slightly simpler, less technical language. Rephrase the question a second time, this time simplifying it even further. Here is an example:

i.   Why might Marxist sociologists be dismissive of secondary education in the United Kingdom?

ii.   What problems might Marxists have with what happens in secondary schools?

iii. What different things that go on in school might Marxists not like?

- Display a question on the board using the terminology which is appropriate for the subject. Spend a short period of time talking about this question to the class. Explain what it means and rephrase once or twice in simpler language. You might like to visually demonstrate the parallels between the rephrased questions and the written questions by pointing to the board as you are speaking.

- Display a question on the board. Ask students to help you rephrase it so that it is simpler. This could be done in a number of ways. Pupils could work in pairs or groups to rewrite the question. A whole-class discussion could be used with various pupils making contributions. Or, you could ask different groups of students to focus on different aspects of the question (such as key words, or clauses), with this then being shared with the class as a whole.

How does it differentiate?

- Rephrasing a question so that a similar meaning is conveyed more simply means that students who are less able or who are less confident with the subject will be provided with another route into the work. If the question is rephrased multiple times (as in the first example above) then there is an increasing chance that all ability levels in the class will be able to access it.

- Initially stating or displaying a question in a more sophisticated form means that, when you are rephrasing it, you will be giving students who do not understand the terminology an opportunity to work out its meaning. They will be able to compare the simpler question with the more complex one and make deductions and inferences as a result. In short, this is scaffolding.
- By starting with the technical form of a question (and then rephrasing it), the teacher is ensuring they challenge all members of the class. Those who are more able will be encouraged to respond in a similarly technical manner. Those who are less able will be challenged to decode the meaning of the question.

14. Bouncing Questions

What does it involve?

Here is an example of what 'bouncing a question' involves:

Teacher: How might the volcano have formed?

Student A: Could it have been caused by the surface bits of the Earth moving?

Teacher: That's a very interesting answer. Student B, what do you think about Student A's answer?

Student B: Well, I remember when we studied earthquakes that we found out that bits of the Earth's surface can move. So maybe by moving they could create a gap that a volcano comes out of.

The teacher poses the question, receives a response and then 'bounces' this response to another student. This avoids an interaction taking place in which all comments flow through the teacher (who comments on them or rephrases them). Instead, the teacher is cultivating a discussion between various members of the class. They are encouraging the students to think actively about what each other have said and to construct knowledge in concert.

In the example above, the teacher could bounce Student B's answer in a number of ways: to Student C, back to Student A, or to the class as a whole. If a discussion begins to develop naturally out of this bouncing, the teacher can step back and facilitate, letting the students take the lead.

How does it differentiate?

- By encouraging students to think about each other's ideas, the teacher is helping pupils to perceive comments made in class as part of a learning process – rather than as items which are fixed and definitive.
- The atmosphere bouncing engenders is a positive one; students are being invited to contribute and to engage with one another's ideas. This helps to draw all students into the lesson.
- 'Bouncing' diminishes the role of the teacher as they move from director of discussion to facilitator of it. This gives students the opportunity to lead their own learning which is, in turn, likely to engage more members of the class.

15. Question Displays

What does it involve?

Display questions or lists of questions around your room. Students can use these to help them with their work. Questions could involve any of the following:

- Questions specific to the subject area being studied
- Questions which students can ask themselves as they are doing their work
- Questions relevant to a particular aspect of students' work (for example, the writing of paragraphs)
- Questions connected to a certain skill (for example, analysing a source)
- Questions concerned with a specific aspect of thinking (for example, evaluation)

These could be used by students while they are engaged in an independent activity, in a group work task, or while they are taking part in a whole-class discussion.

The major advantage of having lists of questions displayed in your room is that students are supported in their thinking. They can look to the lists for ideas, for guidance, or for suggestions as to how they might engage with the information or ideas to hand. In a sense, the displays are prompts.

You might like to develop the use of question displays by working with your students to create them. This could involve an activity wherein groups of pupils are given a heading under which they are to come up with a series of helpful questions. These could then be transferred to a large sheet of paper and decorated, before being put up on the classroom walls.

How does it differentiate?

- Question displays can support students who are struggling with some aspect of the work. They do this by providing prompts which function in much the same way as teacher modelling or scaffolding.
- They can challenge students or stretch their thinking. A question display could contain a series of generic extension questions for students to attempt once they have finished the main activity.
- The displays can encourage students to work independently. Pupils can use them when they get stuck, rather than immediately turning to the teacher for support. This will help students to see themselves as active learners.

Chapter Four - Things you can ask students to do or use

In this chapter we turn the focus onto students by providing fifteen great examples of things they can do or use during lessons.

1. Students Teaching

What does it involve?

There are a number of different ways in which students can take over the role of the teacher. Here are five examples:

- Invite one or more students to come to the front and lead the class in a discussion. One of the advantages of this approach is that it requires little planning. If you choose able and confident students, it is likely that they will be able to lead and manage a debate given nothing more than a starting point in the form of a question or a contentious statement. If you wish to give more support, you can provide prompts in the form of subsidiary questions to ask, aspects to explore or associated topics to move the debate onto. These can be written on a sheet or some small pieces of card and given to the student who is leading the discussion.
- Ask a group of students to plan an activity which they will teach to the rest of the class. This could be used as an extension task, a reward, or as a means of building confidence for the pupils who are involved.
- Divide the class into groups and give each group a topic which they have to research and then teach to the rest of the class. Set a range of success criteria which can act as guidelines regarding the structure of what you are asking pupils to do. An example set of success criteria would be: Ensure everyone in your group has a role; Explain the key points of your topic; Create an activity in which the class can take part; Use drama in

one part of your teaching; Assess whether people have understood what you have taught them.

- Divide the class into groups. Give each group a separate topic or question to research. When sufficient time has passed, explain that one member from of group must act as an envoy. They are to leave their colleagues and to go around the room teaching all the other groups about what they have found out. The activity continues until each envoy has visited and taught each group. Envoys then return to their starting positions and are taught by their colleagues about the rest of the information.

- Include a regular 'show and teach' section in your lessons. Invite students to bring in items, ideas or experiences (the latter two could be represented by an item) which they teach their peers about. You might ask your pupils to bring things in which are connected to the particular subject being studied. If this is the case, the activity will serve as enrichment beyond the classroom as well as something of use and worth within lessons.

How does it differentiate?

- Students share social codes. It is therefore likely that if they are teaching one another they will find information and ideas easier to access than might be the case if everything was coming directly from the (adult) teacher.

- Asking students to teach bestows responsibility and independence on them and. It is therefore confidence-building and engaging.

- Teaching is an active process. It involves the manipulation of information and ideas, such that these can be conveyed in a meaningful and intelligible way to other people. Students who act as teachers – whatever their starting position – will be challenged and will have their thinking stretched because of these inherent requirements.

2. Confidence Indicators

What does it involve?

If you know how confident your students are with the work they are doing, then you are in a strong position. This is because you can adapt your teaching accordingly. If, for example, you know that about a third of your class are struggling to grasp a new concept, then you can set the rest of the class off on an activity and meanwhile do some intensive catch-up work with them. Here are five ways in which you can elicit information from your pupils about how confident they are feeling:

- Thumbs. Ask your students to display their confidence levels to you using their thumbs. If pupils are feeling confident with the work, they give a 'thumbs up'. If they are feeling OK about the work, they show their thumbs pointing horizontally. If they are feeling unconfident about the work, they point their thumbs down.
- Traffic lights. Provide each student in your class with three pieces of card. One piece should be green, one piece should be yellow, and one piece should be red. Ask students to display the card on their desk which represents their confidence level (green = confident; yellow = OK; red = unconfident). This could be done continually through the lesson or at specific points. If the latter, cards could be held up instead of being placed on desks.
- Four corners. Attach a confidence level to each of the four corners of the room (display these on the board so that students can see them). Invite pupils to move to the corner which best represents where they feel they are at. You can then team up confident and unconfident students, ask the unconfident students to work separately with you, or revisit the whole topic (if a large number feel low in confidence).
- Write in books. As a plenary, ask students to write in their books how confident they feel about the work they have done in the lesson. You might ask them to rank themselves on a scale, or

you might provide a list of the key ideas looked at in the lesson and ask them to comment on their confidence levels in relation to each one of these.

- Exit boxes. Create three ballot boxes. Label these: 'confident'; 'OK'; and 'unconfident'. At the end of the lesson, give each student three slips of paper. Ask them to choose three things which have been studied in the lesson and to write these on their slips. As pupils leave the classroom, they should deposit these slips in the boxes which represent their confidence levels about them. The teacher can then collate the results and assess what patterns and trends are apparent in the class as a whole.

How does it differentiate?

- If you know the confidence levels of your students regarding what you are teaching them, then you can adapt your teaching to suit. This means that you will be meeting the various needs of the pupils in your class.
- Students who are less confident can be given extra support by the teacher to help them get to grips with the work.
- Students who are more confident can be given more challenging activities, questions or extension tasks to think about.

3. Expert Corner

What does it involve?

Ask for a student who feels they are an expert in the topic being studied. This pupil sits in a corner of the room. They should be given their own table and two chairs (one for them, one for the students who go up to them). The class is set a task. They are informed that if anyone has any questions or concerns, they should head over to Expert's Corner for help (this being the corner where the student is sat).

While the activity is going on, you can direct your time toward helping students who are most in need of support. Other pupils can make use of the student-expert should they need assistance. You might develop the activity by having two or three experts in different parts of the room. These could all be experts on the topic, or they could experts on different areas of the topic.

It might be the case that the experts do not have many queries. If this happens, the teacher can direct them to do one of three different things:

i.   Create a set of questions which could be used to test what the class knows at the end of the activity, or which could be used as extension questions by those students who finish before their peers.

ii.   Walk around the class and engage various students in discussion. Conversations should centre on aspects of the task and aspects of the topic. The 'expert' could start the discussions off by asking the person to whom they are speaking to talk them through their work thus far.

iii.   Choose a specific aspect of the topic and create a short presentation and teaching activity which can be used with the whole class when the main task has been completed.

How does it differentiate?

- Students have an alternative person to the teacher who they can call on for support. Due to this person being a fellow pupil, there is the likelihood of shared codes making information and ideas easier to access.
- The students who take on the role of expert are challenged to support their peers and to make use of their knowledge and understanding in a variety of different ways.
- The teacher is afforded time in which to support students who are having the greatest difficulty with the work.
-

4. Helpers

What does it involve?

Students work at different speeds. Many factors influence how quickly a pupil completes an activity. These include the nature of the task, the student's prior knowledge and experience, their particular skills and so on. It is likely that in most cases, there will be at least one student who finishes before their peers.

Such pupils can be called upon to act as helpers. The teacher asks them to stand up and to walk around the room, assisting students who have not yet finished. It may be that they take their work with them and use it to help explain ideas and to model what the finished product ought to look like.

As more students complete their work so more helpers are created. Eventually, you can reach a situation where every student who is still striving to finish is being supported by one or more of their peers. This creates a collaborative, positive atmosphere in which pupils see themselves as part of a community that is learning together. It also provides an opportunity for the teacher to circulate and to listen to the conversations which are going on around the room. Through doing this, the teacher can elicit information about where students are at, how they are explaining the ideas and information and whether there are any misconceptions or false assumptions floating about.

How does it differentiate?

- The pupils who become helpers are challenged to support their peers. They must think carefully about how best to convey the knowledge and understanding accrued through successfully completing the task.
- Students are supported by their peers to complete their work. The help they receive is likely to be viewed differently to that which a teacher might give.

- The students who have completed their work and who then become helpers are likely to have a different perspective on the task and the learning to the teacher who has planned and taught the lesson. This is likely to be closer to the experience of those students who they are being asked to help. As such, what they explain and model may well prove more accessible than a similar intervention made by the teacher.

5. Model Answers

What does it involve?

Model answers can come from one of three sources. They can be provided by students, with the teacher collecting examples during the course of the year. They can come from the teacher, who has the skills necessary to construct model answers for any of the work which they ask students to do in lessons. And they can come from examination boards – should you be teaching a course at GCSE or A Level.

Wherever they come from, model answers remain in essence the same. They are a demonstration of how to complete a task or respond to a question. They will not necessarily be the only way, but they will be a model way – that is, a way which meets the success criteria and which the teacher would want their students to follow.

By providing pupils with model answers, you will be helping them to understand what questions and tasks are asking for. To the teacher who has planned the lesson, this is no doubt obvious. To students, however, ambiguity can remain. This is often the case with pupils who are less confident with the work and who are less able in the subject.

Model answers can be used in a number of ways. Here are five suggestions:

- Give each student a copy of a model answer and ask them to read through it and to identify three things which they think are good.
- Students work in pairs. Each pair receives a copy of a model answer. Students read this through. The teacher displays three discussion questions on the board. Pairs work through these questions, making a note of their thoughts in preparation for sharing these with the rest of the class.
- Students work in pairs. Each pair receives a copy of a model answer and a mark scheme. Pairs read through the answer and use the mark scheme to assess it. They should discuss their thoughts until they agree on what they believe to be the correct grading.
- Students work in threes. Each group receives a copy of a model answer. Groups are asked to analyse the model answer and to draw up a set of guidelines which the class could use when they complete the task or question.
- Students work in threes. Each group receives a different model answer. Groups are asked to create a short presentation in which they focus on three of the best things about their model answers – examples and explanation are, of course, obligatory.

How does it differentiate?

- Model answers provide all students with a clearer understanding of what a task or question is demanding. Therefore, they help all students to achieve more than might otherwise be the case.
- Model answers minimise ambiguity for less able and less confident students. They provide a path which these students can follow.
- Model answers give all students an insight into possible ways of ordering, synthesising and communicating ideas and information. Regardless of a students' starting point, they will be able to take something away from a model answer.

6.   Prior Knowledge

What does it involve?

All students arrive at a lesson in possession of prior knowledge. This could have come from:

-   Previous lessons
-   Personal experience (which we will look at specifically in the next entry)
-   Exposure to various forms of media
-   Reading
-   Discussions with family members

and much more besides.

For our purposes here, we can delineate prior knowledge into three categories;

-   That which bears no connection to the topic of study.
-   That which bears a tangential connection to the topic of study.
-   That which bears a direct connection to the topic of study.

The second and third cases are the ones of interest to us. If, as teachers, we can elicit some of this knowledge – or simply get students to recall it and connect it to the lesson in hand – then we are in a position to make what we are teaching more accessible.

By helping students to connect their prior knowledge to the lesson, the teacher provides pupils with a reference point – a means by which to access the learning. It is like putting a flag in a map and saying: 'Right; that is where we are starting from.' As your students progress, they will at all times be in a position to turn around and reference what is going on against that starting point. As such, it gives them a firmer, stronger foothold in lesson. It contextualises the learning and gives it meaning as regards the student's own life.

The best way in which to draw out relevant prior knowledge is through simple starter activities such as listing, open questions, discussion in pairs and as a whole class, matching and spider diagrams.

How does it differentiate?

- Causing students to connect prior knowledge to the lesson in hand makes the learning more accessible.
- All students will come to a lesson with prior knowledge (though this may vary in degree). Therefore, using activities to draw it out will see the teacher working to engage all students.
- Linking something new (the learning to be done in the lesson) with something already known (the prior knowledge) is a way of contextualising and giving meaning to that which is novel. This helps to make it accessible for all pupils.

7. Personal Experience

What does it involve?

Personal experience, despite being touched on in the previous entry, is sufficiently important to warrant a separate treatment.

We noted above that a student's personal experience could be identified as being part of their prior knowledge. This is true in the broad sense that knowledge is the things we know. We might create some nuance however, by further delineating between knowledge gained in formal education and knowledge gained in other settings. In so doing, we are able to cleave that experience which students have in school from the rest of their experience.

This is important on two counts. First, some students may not enjoy school. This could be for a variety of reasons including the possibility that they struggle with academic work and therefore find it difficult to achieve success as it is defined in education (perhaps becoming disengaged as a result). Second, what happens beyond formal schooling is likely to play a larger part in a student's life than vice versa. If we accept this proposition, we can then go on to imagine school as contextualised by the student's wider experience, rather than the other way round.

So, personal experience represents a way to connect learning done in the classroom to the student's own life (thus giving it meaning and making it accessible) and to break down some of the barriers pupils might erect against the codes, language and formalities of schooling.

The teacher should look to include opportunities in lessons for students to bring in their personal experiences. Examples of when this might be appropriate include: during discussion, through the planning of activities based on real-world problems, through the use of activities which explicitly ask students to call upon their personal experiences and through short starter activities which ask students open questions or ask them to connect the topic or key word to their own experiences.

How does it differentiate?

- All students have personal experience. Therefore, this is a technique which has the potential to engage all students.
- Connecting personal experiences to formal learning is a way of contextualising and giving meaning to the latter. This is likely to make the work done in lessons more accessible for students.
- Including opportunities to relate personal experiences in lessons helps to break down some of the barriers to learning pupils may erect in response to past experiences in school.

8. Pace Yourself

What does it involve?

Where possible, set up lessons or segments of lessons in which students are able to go at their own pace. Here are some ways to do this:

- Make use of extensions, stepped activities, options, choices and open activities.
- Create a series of hand-outs which students have to work through. When they finish one hand-out, they come and collect the next one from you.
- Give students a list of things they must do, a list of things they should try to do and a list of things that are 'extras'. Let them work through the lists at their own pace.

It might seem that this entry should be in the section concerned with what the teacher can do. The reason it is here is that it is the student who is doing the thing which is differentiating – they are going at their pace; the teacher is simply facilitating this; they are creating a situation in which it is made possible.

It is advisable for the teacher to share with their students what is going on. This is so that pupils can become aware of their own work-rate and then pace themselves accordingly. You might like to spend a minute or two explaining to your class that you have set up the activity in such a way as to allow people to work at different speeds. This could be caveated by a reminder that you expect all students do their best and that everyone should try to get on as far as possible. In addition, you might like to point out that none of the work is inaccessible to anyone in the class – it is simply that you are aware people work at different speeds and you want to take account of that.

How does it differentiate?

- In any class, there will be students who work at different speeds. Who this is might vary depending on the topic being studied or the type of activity which has been planned. By providing students with the means by which to go at different speeds, you will be ensuring that all members of the class continue to be challenged ad to make progress during the course of the task.

- Responding to the different 'paces' in your class is agile teaching; it sees all students accessing the same work while also operating at a level which is suitable for where they are presently at.
- Students are more likely to experience success if they are in a position to pace their own learning. Those at the lower end of the ability range will avoid feeling left behind and those at the top end will have their thinking continually challenged.

9. Plan First

What does it involve?

Encourage students to plan their wok before they start. Here are the advantages of creating a plan:

- It gives you an opportunity to think about what you want to do and why you want to do it.
- It provides you with a structure which you can then follow.
- By creating a structure in advance, you remove various processes, such as ordering, arranging and designing, from your mind. This frees up your short-term memory to concentrate on the content you are putting into your structure.
- A plan, therefore, acts as an extension of your mind. It is a tool that you can use to help yourself.
- A plan is a reference point which can assist you if you get lost (which is more likely to happen the larger the task which has been undertaken).

It will not always be appropriate to create a plan. Tasks which have a number of elements, which require the creation of a large piece of work, or which require a sustained, consistent response (as in an essay) are those for which a plan will be most useful. However, if you teach your students how to make plans, then they can decide for themselves when they wish to use them.

Here is a set of rules for making plans:

- Keep it simple.
- Divide up the task into smaller sections.
- Work out what each smaller section will involve.
- Make a brief note of this.
- Put the smaller sections into an order.

Two important points for students to remember when using plans are:

- Avoid plans becoming too detailed. They should be a guide to help you with the work.
- Because plans are only a guide, they are not set in stone. If you go off plan or need to change your plan, do not worry. As long as you have a good reason for doing it, that is fine.

How does it differentiate?

- Plans are a tool that all students can use to make difficult or complex tasks easier to complete.
- Plans free up pupils' short-term memory to concentrate on the content they are putting into their work. Therefore, using plans makes tasks more accessible to students.
- If tasks are made more accessible, there is a higher chance that more pupils will be able to achieve success. This will increase their motivation and engagement.

10. Break It Down

What does it involve?

Breaking something down into smaller pieces means that what was once large and potentially unwieldy or difficult becomes simpler and more accessible. Consider a steak. If you try to eat this in one go, it will not be easy. If, however, you cut the steak up into little portions then the whole task becomes an absolute cinch.

Encourage your students to break tasks down into smaller parts so that they might find activities easier to complete. Begin by talking to your pupils about what this process might mean. Demonstrate how to do it using an activity from one of your lessons. Talk students through the differences between tackling something in total and dealing with smaller elements one at a time.

Next, divide students into groups of three. Give each group a piece of paper containing five large or complex tasks. Explain that it is for the groups to work together to break each task down into a series of smaller parts. Indicate that one member of each group should make a note of what is decided upon for each of the five tasks.

When sufficient time has passed, bring all the groups back together and develop a whole-class discussion in which ideas are shared about the breaking down of each of the tasks. Finally, ask each group to produce a paragraph explaining why it is beneficial to break large or complex tasks down into smaller pieces.

This process provides students with an insight into how to break tasks down and also why to break them down. Having done it, students will be in a position to put what they have learnt in practice. This means that the teacher can say to them in future lessons: 'If you are having difficulties or you are not sure how to start, try breaking the task down into smaller pieces – just like we did in groups in our previous lesson.'

How does it differentiate?

- Breaking a large or complex task down into smaller elements means it is easier to do. It is therefore likely that more students will be able to access and complete the work.
- By teaching students how to break tasks down you will be giving them the means to do so on their own. This will increase independence and motivation.
- Giving students a tool with which to simplify the difficult or complex is a way of empowering them, regardless of their starting point. It will also assist them in making progress when faced with challenges in lessons.

11. Ask For Help

What does it involve?

It can be exasperating when you realise a student has been doing nothing for a long period of time. Invariably they will state, when questioned, that they 'did not know what they were meant to be doing,' or that they 'don't understand the task.' If only they had asked for help! If only they had called on the expertise of the teacher! Here are five ways to encourage students to do this:

- Spend time talking to your class about why you are there and what it means to ask you for help. Stress your role as someone whose job it is to support students and to help them to learn. Indicate how this extends to all periods of the lesson but that you need to be told if help is required.
- Model asking for help. This could involve you talking to your class about occasions when you have asked for help. Alternatively, you could seek assistance from your students in explaining ideas or information (particularly those things which are relevant to the experience of youth).

- Give students discreet ways of signalling to you – they may not like the attention that a raised hand draws. Some methods include: traffic light cards; placing a pen across one's book; and sitting with folded arms.
- When you have finished explaining a task, invite the class to ask questions about what is happening and what you are expecting them to do.
- Sit students who are likely to require help in accessible places, such as at the front of the class or around the edge (as in, at the end of a row). This will make it easier for you to go and speak with these students and should minimise any disruption or drawing of attention (which might inhibit students from requesting help).

How does it differentiate?

- He teacher can tailor their assistance to the needs of whoever asks for help. This is personalisation at its best.
- If students ask for help they will not remain stuck or uncertain about what it is they are expected to do. Therefore, more students will be able to access the learning and make progress.
- An atmosphere in which students feel comfortable asking for help will be one in which learning is seen as a collaborative process in which all can be successful.

12. Ask Yourself

What does it involve?

Provide students with a list of questions which they can ask themselves whenever they encounter a task. These could be a set of general questions appropriate for any activity, or they could be specific to a particular type of activity which comes up again and again in your lessons. An example of the latter would be source analysis in History lessons.

When pupils come to begin an activity, they can use the list of questions as a means to structure their work. In addition, cycling through a list of questions each time one completes a task is likely to promote focussed and methodical thinking.

Here is an example of a list of general questions:

- What is the task asking you to do?
- What information will you need to include in your response?
- Can you break the task down into smaller sections?
- What are the success criteria for the task?
- How will you know that you have successfully completed the task?

Here is an example of a list of specific questions, based on source analysis in History lessons:

- Who created the source?
- What might have been the purpose of the source?
- How does the source compare to other sources you know about?
- What key information can you get from the source?
- Is the source biased?

You will note from these two examples that a list of questions works to bridge the gap between where a student is at and where you want them to get through completing the task or activity. The questions assist the pupil by directing their thinking in certain directions. They are more than a prompt yet less than a guide. In a sense, they are akin to a cyclist who leads out their teammate and then drops off in order to let them accelerate away.

How does it differentiate?

- You might choose to give a question list to certain students who you feel need more support than others. This would result in the method differentiating for those who are less able.

- You might create different question lists with different levels of challenge and distribute these to pupils for whom they are appropriate. This will differentiate for all involved.
- You might provide all students in the class with the same question list. This will ensure that all pupils can get to grips with the work. They can then move on at their own pace.

13. Ask Your Partner

What does it involve?

In any classroom, students will be sat next to one another. This provides an opportunity for pupils to use their peers to help them to understand the work. You can cultivate an atmosphere in your classroom whereby students are encouraged to ask their partner should they find themselves unsure about what they are being asked to do or uncertain about some aspect of the learning.

The risk with this method is that it has the potential to be used by students as cover for a social chat. Two ways in which to mitigate this are through the development of a seating plan in which such opportunities are less likely to present themselves and by keeping a close eye on the conversations which take place. Discussions concerning the work tend to look visibly different from social discussions.

Another option is to provide a structure within which students can ask their partners for help. Here are three alternatives:

- Having explained the task which you want students to complete, indicate that there will be a five minute period in which discussion can take place between partners concerning what the task involves and how it might be approached (this is premised on the fact that independent work is to follow).
- Explain to pupils what the activity they are to complete involves. Give a few minutes discussion time in which pairs can

talk about this. Bring the whole class back together and ask if anyone still has any queries or questions. Finally, choose two or three students to relay their understanding of the activity to the rest of the class.

- Part-way through an activity which requires pupils to work independently, invite students to spend one or two minutes sharing what they have done so far with their partners. This gives everyone in the class an opportunity to see how someone else is approaching the task. In addition, it facilitates a discussion about the demands of the task and the possible ways in which these might be met.

How does it differentiate?

- Students may be able to offer their peers a better explanation of what is required by a task due to their shared codes and similar perspectives.
- Encouraging pupils to look to their peers for support helps to create a collaborative learning environment in which success is something which is accessible to all.
- Those students who are asked for support by their peers will be challenged to explain accurately that which they have come to understand.

14. Thinking Aids

What does it involve?

In this chapter there has already been mention of various thinking aids – things which extend students' minds and help them to access the work. Here are a further five thinking aids which you can encourage pupils to use:

- Indexes and glossaries. Both of these are means by which a reader might make swift use of a book for reference purposes.

The former allows one to navigate to specific points while the latter provides definitions for key terms appropriate to the subject matter. Students who use these thinking aids are likely to be more independent. They will begin to see books as items of reference which can be dipped in and out of, rather than as agglomerations of text which are difficult to navigate.

- Words on the wall. Display key words and definitions on the walls of your room. Encourage students to use these to assist them when they are completing their work. This will help pupils to use technical vocabulary and will also act as a memory prompt.
- Dictionaries. The ultimate reference tool for the user of language. Dictionaries offer a significant extension of the mind as they hold information far in excess of what we might be capable of storing individually. In addition, that which is contained in dictionaries is fixed. Therefore, they can be used to check the validity of things which we remember. Finally, dictionaries contain the accumulated knowledge of a culture (or more accurately, a section of that knowledge). This means that there will be much in dictionaries with which students are not yet familiar. By using dictionaries, pupils will broaden their horizons and come across new information.
- Thesauri. You might like to create a little area in your room where a range of dictionaries and thesauri can be stored. Students will then be able to visit this section in order to look up words or to collect a book to take back with them to where they are sitting. Thesauri function in a similar way to dictionaries – they are fixed collections of accumulated knowledge concerning the relationships of similarity and difference between words. They can be used and consulted by pupils in the same way as dictionaries; the benefits which students get from using them are similar in form albeit different in terms of content.
- Textbooks. If a student is stuck as to what something means, if they are sitting there racking their brains about how to explain something, or if they are trying and failing to remember some

point or other, then encourage them to use a textbook – if appropriate – as a means to help. It is much better for a student to produce as much work as possible in a lesson, to the highest standard they can manage, than it is for them to spend time sitting around unable to get on with the task. Textbooks are tools which can be called upon as a means of assistance.

How does it differentiate?

- Thinking aids can do some of the work for students. This helps them to move on in the task, to access the work and to complete everything that has been set.
- Thinking aids extend students' minds. They connect them to some of the accumulated knowledge of their culture. This helps them to do more than they could manage on their own. Therefore, it helps them to learn and to make progress, regardless of their starting point.
- Encouraging students to use thinking aids encourages them to be independent. This is because they are led to see how they might work through difficulties themselves. Students who are more independent will be a better position to access and engage with the work, no matter where they are at in terms of their learning.

15. Have No Fear

What does it involve?

It is better to have a go at something and to learn from what happens then not to have a go at all. Getting students to think in this way is not easy. Many pupils will see the classroom as a zone in which things are either right or wrong, with praise and success attached to the first of these and failure and disapprobation attached to the second. As such, one often finds that a number of students in any one class are reluctant to try new things, push themselves or even, at times, to complete a task which they believe has within it the possibility of failure.

While a lack of fear is something that only students can possess – we cannot give it to them – the teacher is in a position to cultivate an atmosphere in which such a disposition is easier to pick up. Here are three ways in which you can increase the possibility that your students will have no fear:

- Use mistakes as a learning opportunity. When students make mistakes, get something wrong or find themselves talking about something erroneously, thank them for bringing the matter up and launch into a discussion about why they think that and what the right answer or way of thinking actually is, as well as why this is the case. Through doing this, the teacher is putting forward the notion that mistakes are beneficial to individual students and to the class as a whole. Over time, they will come to be seen as great learning opportunities (which are often particularly rich because of the experience of contrast between that which was not correct and that which was).
- Find opportunities to talk about mistakes you have made and demonstrate how you have learnt from these. Easy reminiscences on which to call include your own time at school, your time at university, driving lessons, work, bringing up children (if you have them) and playing sport. By showing that you frequently make mistakes and then learn from them, you will be further normalising the process in the minds of students.
- Give praise at every opportunity (and always for something specific which is linked to the learning) and do not castigate students for making errors. This promotes a positive atmosphere and diminishes the evidence pupils might rely on for their own belief that error will lead to disapprobation.

How does it differentiate?

1. If your students have no fear then they will not be bothered about making mistakes. If they are not bothered about making mistakes then they will be more likely to have a go at all the tasks you set and to engage with the learning.

2. If students recognise mistakes as an opportunity to learn, they will begin to see that learning is not or make or break process. Such a realisation will encourage all pupils to engage with the work (as it changes their perceptions of what success looks like a dhow accessible success is).

3. A positive approach to learning that does not fear error will lead to greater motivation in students. No matter where they start from, pupils who are more motivated are more likely to access the work, to make progress and to put in their maximum effort.

Chapter Five - Things the teacher can do

In this chapter there are resent twenty-five differentiation strategies, activities and techniques based around what the teacher can do while teaching, planning and assessing.

1. Planning Groups

What does it involve?

When using group work, plan who will be in each group in advance of the lesson. This involves sitting down and considering who is in the class, the relative strengths and weaknesses of these students, the prior knowledge you have concerning their behaviour and relationships with one another, and what you want your pupils to get out of the work you are going to set them.

Due to the large number of factors influencing how groups work together, it is not easy to land on winning combinations from the off. In fact, it is likely that you will need to go through a certain amount of trial and error in order to reach a point where you have all your students working successfully. The benefits of persevering are great however.

A group of students working well together is likely to produce work that is far in advance of what the average independent performance of the group members would be. What is more, those students who are less able or less skilled in the topic of study are in a position to learn a great deal from the more able peers with whom they work. A final advantage to note is that pairing students who are enthusiastic with those who are less so can be an effective way of engaging the latter group.

Here are some points to think about while planning groups:

- What sort of combinations are you looking for and why?

- Who would benefit from working together – and how would they benefit?
- What is the purpose of the task and how will putting certain students in the same group help to achieve this?
- What will you do if the groups do not prove successful (or as successful as you hoped)?
- How will you assess the success of the groups?

How does it differentiate?

- Group work differentiates by providing students with opportunities to learn together, to learn from one another, and to use one another for support and help.
- Planning groups in advance means that the teacher can put students together who they think will bring one another specific benefits.
- The teacher can also construct groups with specific aims in mind related to the learning – for example: trying to engage disaffected learners, offering support to those who are less able or giving leadership responsibility to specific pupils.

2. **Explaining and Exemplifying**

What does it involve?

Never underestimate the importance of explanation and exemplification in the classroom. The teacher's job consists of two things: teaching and helping students to learn. To be successful in both of these elements, one must communicate with clarity, precision and accuracy.

There may be more than thirty students in front of you, all of whom need to understand what it is that you are trying to convey to them. The better you communicate, the more likely it is that they will. This, in turn, will increase students' confidence and decrease the amount of time you have to spend going over what you have already said.

Here are a range of methods you can use when explaining things:

- Examples
- Analogies
- Evidence
- Modelling
- Reasoning
- Images
- Diagrams
- Flow Charts
- Stories
- Anecdotes

The first of these – examples – is one of the most important tools a teacher has at their disposal. We will pause briefly to consider why.

Examples give a specific case which demonstrates or supports an abstract or general statement. In so doing, they contextualise that statement. This has three major consequences. First, it provides supporting evidence that the statement is true. Second, it provides an indirect explanation of the statement. Third, it gives the reader or listener purchase – a means by which they can fix onto the statement and connect it to their experience or knowledge of the world.

Here is an example (which is itself an example in reference to the previous paragraph):

Democracy is rule by the people. (General and abstract statement)

For example, voters have the opportunity to elect their representatives every five years. (Example which clearly contextualises the initial statement)

Examples are of great use in the classroom. They help to clarify, demonstrate and support abstract and general statements, giving students purchase on what are often new and sometimes unusual ideas or concepts.

How does it differentiate?

- Thinking carefully about how to explain and exemplify what you say in the classroom means that you are thinking carefully about how to communicate. The better you communicate, the more likely it is that all your students will understand what is being taught and what it is you are asking them to do. This in turn will lead to greater engagement, motivation and progress across the board.
- Giving examples provides students with a means to contextualise abstract and general statements. If you choose your examples carefully, you will be able to use them to engage students and to help all learners access the work.
- Explaining things clearly minimises ambiguity. This increases the chances that all students will understand what is expected of them. Less able students will benefit from this. It is they who are often low on confidence and fearful of getting things wrong. Minimising ambiguity will help them to feel more confident and clearer about what it is they need to do.

3. Modelling Conversation

What does it involve?

Discussion is an important part of good pedagogy. It gives students an opportunity to explore ideas, to make mistakes which can be instantly rectified, to hear the thoughts and ideas of others, to articulate what it is that is in their minds, to build knowledge in conjunction with other people, and much more besides.

In order for students to get the most out of discussion, they need to know what type of talk it is that the teacher wants (and which therefore will most help them learn). The best way to convey this to students is through modelling. Here are three ways in which you can do this:

- Before beginning a discussion task, choose a student who you know is skilled in that area and have a conversation with them about the topic being studied while the rest of the class listens in. Your conversation should proceed in a manner which you want students to imitate. You may decide to stop the conversation at various points in order to highlight certain things for students. Alternatively, you may want to talk about these various points sequentially at the end of the conversation. A final possibility involves inviting pupils to comment on the strengths of the conversation once it is over.
- Throughout your interactions in the classroom, ensure that you are modelling a way of speaking and listening which you want your students to imitate. This might be such as to be clearly differentiated from the kind of speaking and listening which takes place outside of the classroom setting. If there is significant different between the two approaches (inside and outside of the classroom), draw attention to it and talk with your students about why it is the case, what benefits it brings and how it helps teaching and learning.
- During a discussion task, move around the room and observe the various conversations which are taking place. Identify a pair or group who are doing particularly well and, at the end of the activity, invite them to recreate their discussion in front of the rest of the class. You and your students can then start a conversation about why these students exemplify good practice and how everybody can learn from this.

How does it differentiate?

- The quality of students' discussion skills will vary across the class. Modelling good practice is a way of helping all pupils to improve the conversations they have as part of their learning.
- Modelling is very accessible. Students are given a multi-sensory experience which they can take in and analyse first-hand. As such, it is a good way to help all students to develop their speaking and listening skills.
- Discussion in itself is an accessible and engaging pedagogical technique. Therefore, helping students to improve their discussion skills is likely to see progress being made across the board.

4. Seating Plans

What does it involve?

Seating plans involve the teacher deciding how the room will be laid out and where their students will sit. We will look at each of these points in turn.

Here are three possible room layouts:

Rows: **Advantages:** Affords the teacher a high level of control; paired work is easy; those sat on the edge are easily accessible; all students are facing forwards.

Disadvantages: Group work requires rearrangement of desks, chairs or students; hierarchical (although some may see this as an advantage).

Horseshoe: **Advantages:** Discussion is easily facilitated in pairs, groups or as a whole class; teacher can easily access all students; most, possibly all, students are facing forwards; non-hierarchical (although some may view this as a disadvantage).

Disadvantages: The teacher cedes some of their control; some students may not be facing the front.

Groups: **Advantages:** Discussion and group work is easily facilitated; students have a number of peers who they can call on for help; teacher can talk to groups as a whole or access individual students with ease.

Disadvantages: Many students will not automatically be facing the front; teacher cedes control as both they and the group become focuses of attention.

This list is by no means definitive, but it does provide some food for thought. For me, the key question is the degree of control you wish to preserve. If you have a class who are difficult to teach and require a high level of structure, go for rows. If the class are easy to teach, look to groups as a way of maximising the benefits of students working together.

In terms of where students sit, here are some points to consider:

- Do you have students who you know will need more support? If so, you may want to position them in places which are accessible, or even right at the front, close to you.
- Are there certain combinations of students you want to avoid? My rule is: if they have a negative effect on the learning (theirs or other people's), then try to keep them apart.
- Can certain students support one another? This might be in terms of explaining the work, setting a good example, keeping one another on track, working well together or motivating one another.
- Will students remain where they are sat at all times? This will help you to think about what might happen if you ask students

to move, to form groups or if you set a task which is particularly active.

- What prior knowledge do you have? This may come through data which is given to you or through your previous experience of the class or students. Think about how you might use it to help your pupils.

How does it differentiate?

- In terms of the layout of the classroom, certain approaches might suit certain students better. In addition, thinking carefully about how accessible pupils are given your chosen layout means that you will be thinking about how easy it will be for you to help and support them.
- In terms of the seating plan, you can position students so that they can help others or so that they can be helped by others.
- In terms of the seating plan, you can position students so as to give them the best possible chance of engaging with the work. This could include keeping them away from pupils with whom they do not work well, sitting them near to you so that you can support them through the lesson, or simply letting them sit near the board if they struggle to read what is displayed on there.

5.   Photocopy Good Work

What does it involve?

Photocopying good work and then developing tasks around this means that all students in the class are able to see what success looks like. They can take elements of that which is defined as good and use it their own work. This could include ways of manipulating content, ways of communicating ideas, approaches to structuring their work, styles of writing and many other things besides. Here are three activities you might use to get students to engage with the work which you have photocopied:

- Students work in pairs. Each pair is given a copy of the good work. The success criteria or mark scheme which was used to judge the work is either displayed on the board or copies are handed out. Pairs go through the work and identify where different elements of the success criteria have been met. The task concludes with a short sharing session in which various pairs talk through different elements they have identified (this could be accompanied by the work being displayed on the board and the teacher highlighting that which each pair talks about).
- Students work in groups. Each group is given a copy (or two) of the good work. If appropriate, this is blown up onto A3 paper. Groups discuss the work with the express intention of identifying three reasons why it is good. Once they have settled on their three reasons, they must produce a rationale of why each of these reasons means that it is good. The task concludes with groups pairing up and taking it in turns to advocate to each other for their respective reasons (there could be an opportunity for groups to ask questions of one another as well).
- Students work in groups. Each group is given a different aspect of the work to discuss and analyse (if there are a lot of groups, some will need to look at the same aspect). When sufficient time has elapsed, groups pair up and take it in turns to relate what they have found out. The pairings then swap one or two more times (if possible) and the process is repeated. The task is concluded by the whole-class developing a short bullet-point list of the key features of the work which have led it to be classed as good.

How does it differentiate?

- Giving students the opportunity to analyse, examine and discuss work which is defined as good means giving them the opportunity to see what they ought to be aiming for. In turn, this makes it clearer to them what success in the subject or topic looks like.

- Students who are less able are provided with a model they can use to help them improve their own work. This goes some way to bridging the gap between where they are at and where you want them to be.
- All students benefit from discussing that which makes a piece of work good. This is because, no matter where any individual student is at, they will be made to think carefully about what their work is being judged against. This causes achieving highly and making progress to be made simpler and more accessible.

6. Evaluate and Create

What does it involve?

Evaluation and creation are two of the harder things we ask pupils to do in the classroom. As such, they offer many opportunities for challenging students and for stretching their thinking. We will look at each in turn, providing a brief analysis followed by a series of practical suggestions.

Evaluation involves the making of a judgement. In order to do this one must have a certain amount of understanding of that which is being judged, as well as that which is being used to make the judgement (the criteria which the judgement refers to). The better one understands both the criteria and the thing itself, the more likely it is that the judgement will be clear, persuasive and nuanced. Here are three ways in which you might use evaluation to challenge students:

- Create tasks or ask questions which require pupils to make a judgement. These could be part of the main task, or they could be extensions which students come onto as a challenge or reward for completing the core work. Examples of words which can be used to structure evaluation tasks or questions include: assess, appraise, critique, judge and rank.
- Challenge students to identify and explain what it is that they are using when they make a judgement. So, for example, if you

are studying World War Two and a student has just finished evaluating a source, you would ask them to identify and explain what it is they used to judge the strengths and weaknesses of the source. This could then lead onto further evaluation – of the criteria the pupil identifies.
- Give students a judgement for which they must develop a defence. This works particularly well if it is something which is unusual, unlikely or that the student does not agree with. The process here involves working backwards. The evaluation has been made, now sufficient reasons for suggesting why it is so need to be found. As such, students are being asked to think in a way which is slightly differently from standard evaluation tasks.

Creation involves the development of that which is new. This might come through the forging of connections, the synthesis of separate items or the application of the imagination to that which already exists or which one already knows (not all things we know also exist). It is difficult. It is much easier to stick with what there is already than it is to attempt to create something which, heretofore, happened not to be the case. Here are three ways in which you might use creation to challenge students:

- Ask students to make and explain connections between that which you are studying and other areas of the curriculum or elements of their experience. You might like to encourage pupils to begin by looking for simple or obvious connections and then challenge them to develop those which are more esoteric or tangential. In this latter case, the key point is that students must be able to explain how they came to forge the connection. As long as they can do this, anything goes.
- Challenge students to create something using that which they have learnt during the lesson. This could be a poster, an advertisement or a newspaper article, for example. In each of these cases, the act of creation involves the drawing together of separate items under the auspices of a given structure. Another

possibility involves asking students to create something which is more of a synthesis. This will be an item which stands on its own yet stems directly from things which are prior. Examples of this would include a story, an argument or a poem.

- Ask students to create an alternative version of something. Examples of what this might be include: the lesson, a part of the lesson, an event, a conversation or a piece of text. You might like to structure the activity by giving pupils some guidelines (so that it is better; for a group of seven year-olds) or a set of success criteria. On the other hand, you might prefer to give students complete free rein on account of the fact that the task is a creative one and the fewer restrictions the better.

How does it differentiate?

- Both evaluation and creation require high level thinking and a good command of the relevant ideas and information. Therefore, questions and activities based around these processes are a sure way of challenging students and of stretching their thinking.

- Evaluation causes student to think critically about that which they have studied. This is challenging because it involves an active reassessment of that which one has already processed. In addition, it pushes students to go beyond simply assimilating knowledge.

- Creation causes students to think about that which they have learnt in new and imaginative ways. As such, they will be pushed to manipulate that which they know and understand and to look at it from a different perspective. Doing this usually proves challenging.

7. Blooming Questions

What does it involve?

Bloom's Taxonomy of Educational Objectives orders the standard elements of cognitive processing that teachers ask students to do in the classroom. The taxonomy runs as follows, from least to most challenging: Knowledge; Comprehension; Application; Analysis; Synthesis; Evaluation. Subsequent research has suggested that the last two categories ought to be swapped over. This is not too important for us here – we can sleep easy with the knowledge that synthesis and evaluation are the two most difficult of the cognitive processes.

Using the taxonomy to inform and structure the questions you use in the classroom is a good way to differentiate. Here are three specific approaches you might like to try:

- When giving students a set of questions which they are to answer as part of an activity, use Bloom's Taxonomy to ensure that they get progressively more challenging. Here is an example:

What is a definition of democracy? **(Knowledge)**

What is the meaning of democracy? **(Comprehension)**

Can you name two countries that are democracies and explain how you know that they are? **(Application)**

What are the key features common to all democracies? **(Analysis)**

How might you alter the political system in the United Kingdom so that it is more democratic? What would your changes look like? **(Synthesis)**

To what extent do you agree that democracy is the best political system which exists? **(Evaluation)**

- Use the taxonomy to structure the questions you ask students during discussion. If you want to challenge a pupil, ask them a higher-level question. If a student is less able, ask them a question from one of the lower stages. You might also like to ask a series of question which gradually ascend the taxonomy. This is a good way of developing the confidence of a pupil who feels they are struggling with the work. A series of correct answers to more concrete questions will aid them in having a go at an abstract, higher-level question.
- One way to plan lessons is to break the time down into smaller segments and assign a question to each segment. These then form the basis of the various periods of the lesson, with the activities the teacher plans helping students to develop appropriate answers. Bloom's taxonomy can be used to underpin the questions which head each section; as the lesson progresses, so the questions move up the taxonomy, getting a little bit more complex each time.

How does it differentiate?

- The taxonomy orders cognitive processes from least to most difficult. Therefore, using it to structure questions means the teacher can tailor what they ask to the particular needs of individual students.
- By gradually working up the taxonomy (in a question set, in discussion, or through the course of a lesson), the teacher is likely to challenge all students, enabling them to make progress no matter their starting position.
- Using more concrete, lower-level questions is a good way to help students who are less able to access the work. The success they experience through this will increase their engagement

and motivation, as well make them more confident about attempting higher-level questions.

8. Top, Middle and Bottom

What does it involve?

It is commonly held that teachers of mixed ability classes 'teach to the middle'. This means that during those periods when they are talking to the class, for example when they are explaining, asking questions or teaching new ideas or information, they pitch the content and their speech to what they perceive as the middle level of ability. This is understandable and, based on the premise that a teacher is trying to reach as many students as possible at the same time, is logically sound. Most classes of this type will contain a range of students whose ability levels are distributed roughly in the shape of a bell curve.

It is quite reasonable for the teacher to 'teach to the middle' as a default option. This is because they can be sure of reaching the most students. If the go below the middle, it is likely that most of the class will disengage because the work is too easy. If they go above the middle, it is likely that most of the class will find it difficult to follow all of what is said.

So, as a rule, teaching to the middle – during the periods when you are talking to the whole class for some particular purpose – is reasonably sound. Teacher talk will probably only make up a small proportion of your lessons – the rest of the time you will be using the strategies outlined in this book to ensure all sections of the class are learning, being challenged and are making progress.

Even so, it is still worthwhile trying to differentiate during periods when you find yourself 'teaching to the middle.' This is easily done. Simply throw in a few sections from time to time when you 'teach to the bottom' and when you 'teach to the top'. Avoid these going on for too long so as to prevent pupils from drifting away or struggling to follow that which is being said. You might like to preface your points with lines such as: 'Now, I know this is going to sound really basic, but I just want to go over it to make sure we're all on the same track,' or, 'This next bit is pretty complicated – but stay with it because it's going to be worth it.'

How does it differentiate?

- Teaching to what you perceive to be different ability levels in the class helps to engage these different groups of students.
- 'Teaching to the bottom' from time to time helps to draw those students who are least able into what is going on. In addition, it frees up time later on when you do not have to support these pupils as much as might otherwise be the case.
- 'Teaching to the top' from time to time helps to engage the most able students and also provides the class as a whole with something which is more challenging.

9.   AfL

What does it involve?

AfL stands for Assessment for Learning. This refers to the way in which teachers can use the process of assessment to help students to learn. It differs from assessment of learning. This is a summative process in which students are tested to see what they have learnt. A good way to understand the difference is to think about a driving lesson and a driving test. In a driving lesson assessment for learning is being used. The instructor looks at what you are doing and helps you to learn how to improve. In a driving test the instructor assesses whether or not you meet a set of pre-defined criteria.

Assessment for learning consists of three key elements:

- Eliciting information from students and using this information to adapt teaching.
- Opening up the process of assessment through peer-assessment, self-assessment and the provision of success criteria.
- Providing formative feedback. That is, feedback which explains what students have done well and what they need to do in order to improve (ideally with explanation of why both happen to be the case).

We will briefly consider what each might involve.

The first case can take many forms. Listening to students, reading their work and observing them in class are all basic ways of eliciting information. Other methods include asking open questions, requesting justification and explanation and setting up activities in which students are doing things. In addition to all this, there are whole-class feedback techniques. These include getting students to write answers on mini-whiteboards, showing with their thumbs how happy or confident they are with the learning and collecting exit passes from students as they leave your lesson (on which they will have written an answer to a question).

The second case involves building peer- and self-assessment into your lessons as well as sharing success criteria or mark schemes with your students. Many activities can be developed which revolve around any of these three processes. In addition, any discussion about mark schemes and assessment criteria is likely to be beneficial.

The third case involves analysing what students have done well in their work and why, what they need to do next if they are to improve and why this will be an improvement and giving this information to students in such a way that they can understand it and act on it.

How does it differentiate?

- Eliciting information from students differentiates because it means the teacher can adapt their teaching to meet the needs of their pupils. This could involve a single student, a group, or even the whole class.
- Opening up success criteria differentiates because it helps students to become aware of what it is that is being expected of them, or what it is that will cause them to experience success in the subject or topic. Therefore, it is a way of helping all students to make progress.
- Formative feedback differentiates because, no matter where a student is at, the teacher will be able to explain to them what they have done well (building confidence and increasing motivation) and how they can get better (ensuring progress).

10. Modelling

What does it involve?

Modelling involves the teacher demonstrating to students what it is they want them to do or what it is that a concept or ideas means. Here are some examples of what this might entail:

i.   The teacher demonstrates the different stages a student will have to go through in order to complete a task. For example, they move around the room, indicating all the different activity stations pupils are expected to visit.

ii. The teacher demonstrates how to do an element of a task. For example, they model the dramatic interpretation of a concept (with this being an element of a wider drama-based task).

iii. The teacher demonstrates the meaning of an idea which they have first stated and then explained. For example, they model an explosion using their hands in order to demonstrate a volcanic eruption.

The major benefit of modelling is that it clearly exemplifies that which the teacher is seeking to convey through speech or writing. It therefore does the following:

- Acts to minimise ambiguity by showing definitively what the teacher's words are intended to mean.
- Offers an alternative route of explanation, thus increasing the chances that students will understand some – or all – of what the teacher is trying to convey.
- Contextualises that which is abstract. This means that those students who find abstract thought more difficult to deal with have a route to understanding which is more suited to their needs.

It will not always be appropriate or necessary to use modelling. However, it is a very helpful tool for the teacher to have in their arsenal. If you find yourself in the position where you have finished speaking and your class are looking at you seemingly nonplussed, repeat what you have just said and supplement it with appropriate modelling. It is likely that you will hear the words 'Oh, now I get it,' not long after.

How does it differentiate?

- Modelling provides a clear demonstration – often visual – of what it is the teacher is trying to convey through words. The alternative route to understanding increases the chances that most students will grasp what is being said.
- Modelling contextualises abstract statements, making them more accessible to students who struggle with that type of thinking.
- Modelling minimises ambiguity (whether this has been created by the teacher or caused by the student). This, in turn, makes pupils more confident as they feel they know what they need to do (and so they do not fear making a mistake).

11. Challenge

What does it involve?

Throughout this book various entries have talked about challenging students. Here are five approaches, not mentioned elsewhere, which you might use to stretch your pupils' thinking:

- **Insoluble problems**. Much of philosophy centres on problems which appear to be insoluble. Use these to challenge students. While they may not come to a definitive answer, they will certainly develop their understanding in the process. Examples of some insoluble problems: Can we prove God does or does not exist? What is art? Can security and freedom coexist? What is the nature of the mind? Do we have free will? Are some judgements better than others?
- **Articles**. Laminate newspaper, internet or magazine articles which are relevant to the subject or topic you are teaching. Keep these close to hand and, when a student finishes the main work before the rest of the class, let them choose one of these to read and analyse. You might supplement the article with a set of questions. For example: What is the main argument? Is the text bias? How might you argue against the content of the article? Why might this article be something which made the news in the first place?
- **This or That**. Give students a difficult choice and ask them to decide on and justify a course of action. Extend the activity by asking for a critique of the opposite course of action.
- **Translation**. Ask students to translate something from one medium into another while retaining as much of the original's meaning as possible. For example, during a lesson on Jane Eyre, you might ask a student to translate one of Mr Rochester's speeches into an image.
- **Perspectives**. When a student finishes their work before the rest of the class, challenge them to reimagine it from a different perspective. The point of view which you or the students

choose will depend on the nature of the work. An example would be as follows. In a lesson looking at human rights, pupils might have been asked to write an essay on what single right is most important. Students could then be challenged to write as if they thought another right was more important, as if they thought no rights were important, or as if they thought the original right they chose was in fact unimportant.

How does it differentiate?

- Specific challenge tasks can be used as extensions to stretch the thinking of the most able students.
- They can also be used as extensions which the whole class strives to try and reach. Such a situation can be achieved by lauding those who get onto the tasks and by creating an atmosphere of excitement around students' attempts to get to grips with them.
- Careful planning of challenge tasks will ensure that they are accessible – while still remaining difficult – for all students. The key difference will come in the work which pupils create in response, with students making progress relative to their various starting positions.

12. Different Media

What does it involve?

A wide variety of media exist which can be used in the classroom, including:

- Television programmes or films.
- Cartoons.
- Radio programmes.
- Songs
- Internet sites.

- Interactive games.
- Books.
- Worksheets.
- Articles.
- Images.

Calling on a selection of media over the course of a term, a year or even a scheme of work means you will be providing students with a variety of ways by which to access information and ideas. There are three key benefits of this.

First, by using a range of media you will be increasing the chances that all pupils in your class will find a medium (or more) which suits them well and through which they can come to understand ideas and information with ease. Second, variety is a good in itself in the classroom. It helps to raise engagement and keep up motivation during a wider experience which is highly circumscribed and repetitive in terms of form, if not in terms of content. Third, the medium is the message. Using a range of media means that you will be presenting students with ideas and information which are conveyed and structured differently. There is often a qualitative difference in the communication which takes place through one medium as compared to another. For example, consider what a television programme can do in comparison to a book – and, indeed, vice versa.

A good way to incorporate a variety of media into a single lesson is through the use of activity stations (as outlined in the chapter on activities). This entails having information conveyed at various stations through various mediums. For example, you might have a laptop set up playing a video, another one set up playing a song, a collection of postcards at a third station, an article at a fourth, a collection of large, glossy photographs at a fifth, a laptop running an interactive game at the sixth and a book at the seventh. While this takes a little bit of time to plan and set up, the benefits are likely to be high – in terms of engagement, motivation and learning.

How does it differentiate?

- Different media will play to different students' strengths. By using a range you will be doing your best to engage pupils, giving them various opportunities to connect with the subject content.
- Variety is likely to increase motivation which, in turn, will increase the chances of students engaging and making progress.
- Different mediums allow information to be conveyed and structured in different ways. Some students may find it easier to assimilate knowledge in certain of these ways than in others.

13. Narrative

What does it involve?

Story-telling is an excellent tool for creating engagement, contextualising concepts and explaining what things mean. In addition to all this, stories which have a human element to them (and most do) give students a point of reference with which they can identify. Here are five ways in which you can use narrative in order to differentiate:

- Concepts, by their nature, are abstract. When introducing students to new concepts, you can use narrative in order to bring them down to a more concrete level. This will help all pupils to gain purchase and understanding; those students who struggle with abstract thinking will benefit the most. An example would be a lesson looking at the concept of justice. This could be contextualised through a story about an individual's fight to overturn a miscarriage of justice.
- Stories can be an excellent way of getting students into a new topic. Of particular note here are stories conveyed through films. The multisensory experience increases the story's effect on those watching and immediately draws students into the world of the storyteller.

- Tell a story to your class in order to explain a key point or to convey an important piece of information. By putting that which you want students to know into a narrative form, you will most likely make it more memorable for pupils then would otherwise be the case. This is a point which has held true over time. Examples of storytellers conveying messages include the Buddha, Jesus and Martin Luther King Jr. to name but a few.
- Build a clear narrative into your individual lessons and across a scheme of work. Make students aware of this and then use it to help them situate where they are (in terms of their learning) and where it is that they are going.
- An important element of story-telling is drama. When using narrative to explain things or to contextualise ideas, make use of drama in order to further engage students and to heighten the tension which is present in what you are doing. Dramatic techniques include pausing, use of the body, altering the speed, tone and volume of one's voice, facial expression and irony.

How does it differentiate?

- Narrative can present complex or abstract information in a way that is easier to access and simpler to understand. It is therefore a means by which to help all students come to terms with the content of the lesson.
- Contextualising ideas through narrative helps students to locate information within their own worldview and life experience. This in turn makes it easier for them to assimilate and interact with that information.
- The dramatic element of storytelling is a good way to engage all students, but particularly those who struggle to cope with information and ideas which are abstract, complex or extensive.

14. Talk To Me

What does it involve?

If you talk to students then it is highly likely you will be differentiating. If you aim to talk to as many students as possible in every lesson (or all your students across a series of lessons), then you will be going a fair way to ensuring everyone in the class is supported and everyone, at least to some extent, is catered for.

When we speak to someone we listen to what it is they say. In addition, we observe their body language and their facial expressions, hear the tone of their voice and pick up on other non-verbal cues. All this is information which we use when we are making our responses. As a teacher, you will be particularly sensitive to these aspects of your students' communication. It will lead you to think carefully about what it is you are going to say to students and how exactly you are going to say it.

The conversations which take place in the classroom between you and your pupils will thus see you tailoring your speech in order to meet their needs. For example, if you observe a student who appears disengaged, you might make an extra point of being upbeat and enthusiastic. On the other hand, a pupil who is struggling to understand the work might be given a series of carefully worked explanations covering the key points which they need to know.

The overall message is clear. Talk to the students in your class and, in so doing, you will find yourself tailoring your speech to meet their needs. As such, you will be differentiating.

How does it differentiate?

- Talking to your students means that you find out where they are at and any difficulties they are having.
- Talking to your students means that you will be tailoring your own speech to meet their needs. As such, you will be

responding to them in accordance with where they are at and will be providing them with the support they need in order to make progress.

- Talking to your students helps to engage and motivate them. It makes it clear that you are interested not just in what they think, but in them as a person. It shows that you are prepared to give your time so as to help them individually.

15. Humour

What does it involve?

Humour is a powerful tool for engaging students and creating a positive atmosphere in the classroom. Everybody likes to laugh and adept use of jokes or slapstick is a good way of lifting the mood and getting pupils onside. Of course, one does not want humour to take over the classroom. If this happens then it is likely that learning will have been displaced as the main focus of the lesson; such a situation is likely to have detrimental effects. Here are three specific ways in which you can use humour to differentiate:

- At the start and end of lessons. If you begin with a little bit of humour – such as a couple of puns or a humorous story – then you will be getting students onside from the word go. The obvious benefit is that this will result in an easier transition into the rest of the lesson. Ending with a little bit of humour means that pupils will leave the room with this lodged in their minds as their final memory of the lesson. Therefore, they will leave with a positive and happy association. This will help keep them motivated and enthusiastic when next they return.
- Unexpectedly. Much humour plays on our expectations – what we think is going to be the case turns out not to be so and we find this funny. For example: A man walks into a bar. 'Ouch!' he says. It was an iron bar. You can use this to your advantage

when teaching by bringing forth the unexpected in your classroom. Two methods which you might like to use are as follows: First, have an image or slide in your presentations which is surprising and in some way humorous. Make no mention of this before it appears in front of students, then appeared shocked as if you didn't know it would be there. Second, make a joke seemingly at random during some part of the lesson when the class's attention is fixed upon you. One-liners and puns are particularly good for this. You might even like to supplement your delivery with a stony face – indicating a knowing irony about the standard and status of the joke.

- Self-deprecation. This is when you make yourself the subject of the joke. Done well, it gets students onside and bridges the gap between teacher and pupils which at other times is a necessary part of teaching. You might say that it humanises you in front of the students.

How does it differentiate?

- Humour creates a positive atmosphere. It is therefore likely to enthuse, engage and motivate the students in your class.
- Humour provides a break in the usual flow of the lesson. It is likely that students who find learning difficult will particularly welcome this. You will be giving them a little light relief. In turn, they will be energised and ready to keep working through the rest of the lesson.
- Humour helps students to see you as a real person. It is therefore possible that it will break down some of the barriers that disengaged students may put up between themselves and the teacher.

16. Listening Frame

What does it involve?

A listening frame is a simple tool which can be of great benefit in helping students to make notes and to process verbal information. It comes in many forms but, in essence, involves a structure through which pupils can record and analyse that which they hear.

Listening frames assist students in two key ways. First, they break down what it is that is being said. The frame contains a series of categories which relate to the speech which is to come. Therefore, pupils can look at the listening frame and anticipate the different elements of the speech. Second, they provide a structure in which pupils can make notes. By indicating the various elements of the speech, the listening frame is also indicating the various elements on which students are expected to take notes.

Here are three worked examples of listening frames which exemplify these points:

- The lesson is on the American Revolution. The teacher is using a sound recording of an actor playing the part of a British soldier sent over to America to help quell the uprising. The listening frame consists of a sheet of paper with a series of questions written on it at roughly equal intervals. There is space in which to write beneath each of these. The subject of each question is indicative of sequential parts of the speech: Who is the speaker and where are they from? What does the speaker think about the uprising? What instructions has the speaker been given? What does the speaker think will happen in the future?
- The lesson is on tourism. The teacher is using a section of a documentary, the whole of which was originally screened on a national television channel. The listening frame consists of a piece of paper divided in four. In each segment there is a question relating to a different character that will feature in the

clip: How has tourism affected Manuel? What impact has tourism had on Silvia's business? What does the environmentalist say about the increase in tourism in the area? How does the politician defend his party's record in the area?

- The lesson is on Macbeth. The teacher is using an extended clip from a radio interview with the director of a recent revival of the play at the National Theatre. The listening frame consists of a piece of paper split into three sections. In each section there is a heading: How has the director altered the play for a modern audience? What does the director think about Shakespeare's use of language? Why does the director think that audiences will be surprised by her interpretation?

How does it differentiate?

- Some of the work is done for students. The listening frame provides the structure and the areas of focus. This means that pupils can concentrate on analysing and assimilating the information.

- The listening frame is a support for students; it takes the pressure off and lets them focus on one thing in turn – the series of questions or statements which form part of the frame. This is of particular benefit to less able pupils who might find the demands of analysing oral information difficult.

- Students can make use of the notes they make in their later work. This means that they will not have to remember everything that was said – a task that will be difficult for many.

17. Extensions

What does it involve?

Extension tasks or questions are a simple way of differentiating any segment of a lesson. They consist of something which is additional to the main work and which pupils attempt once they have finished the primary activity. You might like to introduce further extensions – I call them super-extensions, hyper-extensions and outer space extension – for students to tackle when they have finished the first extension. Here are five examples of generic extensions which you could use in almost any lesson:

- **Set students a task which has to be completed inside a strict and challenging time limit**. The time pressure will push pupils to think quickly and carefully; they will have less opportunity to ponder possibilities and will have to make sound and accurate decisions in a prompt manner.
- **Ask students to write an exam question based on what they have been studying, as well as a mark scheme which could be used to assess responses**. If only one pupil has finished the primary task, invite them to write an explanation of their question and of their mark scheme. They should indicate how they went about creating them and why they feel they are good. If a second student is on the extension task, ask the two of them to have a go at each other's exam questions.
- **Display a further question on the board which students are to attempt once they have finished the main activity**. These questions should be distinctly harder than that which has constituted the primary task. As such, you might use key words from the top two levels of Bloom's Taxonomy to create the questions. Alternatively, you might ask philosophically-inclined, conceptual or abstract questions. Another option is to pose questions which are counter-intuitive or which cause students to look again at what they have studied (for example, more

critically, from a different perspective or through a different conceptual framework).

- **Provide students with a mark scheme and ask them to assess their own work**. This will only be possible if you have a mark scheme or a set of success criteria available. Ask pupils to identify what they have done well and what they need to do to improve. Students should explain in detail why they have made their judgements. In particular, they should refer to the criteria which they have sued. As a final point, pupils can redo their work taking account of the possible improvement they have noted.

- **Ask students to create a poem based on something they have studied during the lesson**. You might like to provide pupils with a structure to follow, for example: Haiku, limerick, rhyming couplet, acrostic or sonnet. The difficulty here comes from having to synthesise that which has been learnt and fit it into a specific literary form.

How does it differentiate?

- Extensions provide a challenge to all students who finish the main activity. They are therefore having their thinking stretched while the remainder of the class are completing the work.

- Extensions that are fun and challenging will engage and motivate students; they will want to finish the main activity so that they can get onto them. Therefore, they help all pupils to make progress.

- If you append an extension to all the activities you plan as part of your lesson, you will ensure there are regular opportunities for your most able students to be challenged. It is likely that this will help keep them engaged and motivated.

18. Check Sheets

What does it involve?

Check sheets provide pupils with a list of things they need to do for a particular task.

Such an item could be created for any piece of work which you ask students to complete. They break down the structure of a task such that pupils are presented with a series of separate elements which they can work their way through. This makes a large, complex or difficult piece of work easier to complete. It is akin to the old saying 'taking one thing at a time.'

There are three possible options for using check sheets:

- Give one to each student in the class and ask them to fill it in as they go along.
- Give one to those students who struggle (or who you think will struggle) with the task in hand.
- Display one on the board during the course of the activity and indicate that pupils can use it as a point of reference, or that they can make a copy in their books which they then fill in as they go along.

How does it differentiate?

- By breaking down a complex task into separate elements, check sheets make it easier for students to complete the work.
- Students who are less able may struggle to find a way into large or complex tasks. If they struggle to get started it is possible they will become disengaged. Check sheets prevent this from happening, increasing the possibility that all pupils will make good progress.
- Check sheets provide a point of reference throughout the course of an activity. This means that students will never become lost or uncertain of what it is they are meant to be

doing (or what it is they need to do next). Again, this will increase the possibility that all pupils in the class will be able to make good progress.

19. Celebrate Mistakes

What does it involve?

Making mistakes is an inevitable part of life and one of the main ways in which we learn. In school, many students are fearful of error. There are a number of reasons behind this.

First, there is the fear of embarrassment. Students may be concerned that they will look foolish in front of their peers. They may believe that they will be made fun of if they make a mistake or that it will reflect badly on them. Pupils may prefer to avoid taking risks in order to play it safe and minimise the chance of failure.

Second, summative assessment has a significant role in school life. This sees students being assessed in order to find out how much they know and understand. Results are given in the form of grades, levels or marks. Such a system inevitably ranks pupils in relation to one another. In addition, the tests which form these types of assessments are high-stakes: there is one opportunity and that is it. These various points, taken together, intimate why it is that students are wary of making mistakes.

Third, pupils may seek to protect their own ego by avoiding situations where a mistake could be made. By ego I refer to that vision of oneself that each of us possesses. If a student has regularly experienced failure in school and does not believe they are capable of accessing the learning which takes place there, they may well become reluctant to put themselves in a position (for example by answering a question) where further failure might be possible. This is akin to a withdrawal. The student disengages in order to preserve their own self-image, or they develop a self-image which is set in opposition to education and those things which are associated with it.

Celebrating mistakes is one way of trying to overcome these barriers. It is a means of turning the fear of failure on its head. It involves praising the mistakes students make as great learning opportunities – and then using them as such.

For example, in a lesson on long division, a student may make a mistake in their working out. Rather than drawing a cross next to this and telling the pupil it is wrong, the teacher can instead ask the student to explain their reasoning and then discuss with them how they went wrong, why they went wrong and how they can learn from this in the future. The teacher could conclude the conversation by thanking the pupil for making the mistake and pointing out that, had they not done so, much less learning would have taken place.

How does it differentiate?

- Many students fear failure in lessons. This discourages them from attempting to answer questions, from completing tasks or from getting involved in activities. Celebrating mistakes is a way of overcoming this.
- An atmosphere in which mistakes are celebrated and used as learning points is likely to be one in which more students engage with the learning.
- Using mistakes as a learning point is an excellent way of helping students to make progress. It does not matter where a pupil is at, they will be able to learn from their mistakes. The approach will therefore bring benefits to all students, no matter their starting position.

20. Coaching (Formative Marking)

What does it involve?

We have already touched on formative marking in the entry on assessment for learning. Here we will look at it in greater detail, as well as consider why it can usefully be thought of as coaching.

Formative marking involves providing students with information about what they have done well and what they need to do in order to improve. At its best, it should reference this to the criteria against which pupils' work is being judged and give an example or demonstration of what improvement will look like (or an explanation of why that stated as an improvement will actually be an improvement). Here is an example:

Strengths: You have explained your reasoning in detail. This has made you argument clear.

You have used technical vocabulary throughout your work, showing you knowledge and understanding of the subject.

Your conclusion is unexpected but supported by the evidence you have outlined. This makes your essay memorable whilst maintaining coherence.

Target: Provide criticisms of the arguments you personally agree with, as well those with which you disagree. This will demonstrate consistent evaluation and a critical mind-set – one which is not biased in favour of one viewpoint or another. Such an approach is preferable as it more closely matches the scientific nature of the discipline.

Of course, this example is extensive and you will not be able to provide such detailed feedback every time you mark. Nonetheless, it does illustrate the points raised above.

You will note that the concept of coaching could be applied to this feedback. What has been offered is a means by which to move on a little bit, by which to get better and through which to learn some more about the subject and the skills which it demands. This is what a coach does; they assess performance and give advice on how to get better.

Formative feedback – viewing marking as a form of coaching – is a means to differentiate. Students in a class will all be at different stages in terms of their learning. Assessing their work in this way will help them all to make progress, regardless of where they are at. The same simply cannot be said for the assigning of a mark, level or grade.

How does it differentiate?

- Formative marking provides all students in a class with the means to make progress, regardless of where they are at in terms of their learning.
- Conceiving of marking as akin to coaching helps teacher and student to view it as a supportive learning-centred process. This increases motivation and engagement as pupils feel they are being helped and do not experience the sense of failure which summative assessment often brings.
- Formative marking is, by definition, closely tailored to the need of individual students.

21. Re-Explain

What does it involve?

We have already considered explanation and exemplifying in a separate entry. Here we will look at a specific method of explaining which helps all pupils to access the learning. It works as follows:

First, explain using technical and subject-specific terminology. Then, simplify your explanation, replacing some of these words with language with which students will be more familiar. Finally, explain a third time, on this occasion actively seeking to use very simple and non-technical language. You might like to visualise the approach as a spiral, with your explanation moving from a technical, abstract and challenging starting point down to a simpler, more grounded and concrete finishing point.

The major advantages of this method are:

- All students are exposed to correct terminology and technical vocabulary. This is challenging for the whole class and also meets the needs of those students who are most capable.
- Students who struggle to grasp the technical and subject-specific language are given an opportunity to come to terms with these words by comparing them to the simpler explanations they hear. Through this process they can deduce the meaning of the first set of words, or, at the very least, develop their understanding of them.
- Pupils who have the greatest difficulty in your lessons will be catered for. They will also be given an opportunity to develop their vocabulary and understanding through making comparisons between the various levels of explanation which you give.

If used all the time this method might grate with your students; it will become formulaic and repetitive. A better option is to use it sporadically, perhaps focussing on those occasions when you are teaching something which is of great importance; something which it is vital that all students comprehend. Specifically, this is likely to involve concepts which are being introduced for the first time and which pupils will need to grasp if they are to make progress through the rest of the topic or unit of work.

How does it differentiate?

- Multiple explanations are aimed at the range of ability levels one is likely to find in any mixed-ability class.
- By using technical vocabulary and subject-specific terminology in the first explanation, you will be challenging all students and giving them the opportunity to engage with the key content.
- Combining the first explanation with the second and third gives students the opportunity to deduce the meaning of words with which they are not familiar. Students are helped to use what they already know to come to terms with that which is unknown.

22. Modelling Thinking

What does it involve?

In every lesson that we teach we are expecting and encouraging students to think. But what do we mean by this? To what does the word 'think' actually refer?

I would argue that it is a catch-all term which can be delineated into a number of different processes. These include such things as recalling, analysing, examining, critiquing and so on. Passing back momentarily to Bloom's Taxonomy – as outlined above – we might take on board that demarcation of processes and thus describe cognitive thought as being divisible into six broad categories (knowledge, comprehension, application, analysis, synthesis and evaluation), each of which contains its own gradations. In so doing we are pointing to the primacy of logico-linguistic thinking in the classroom. While this is not the be all and end all – and particularly in terms of differentiation we would want to open up a number of areas of thinking such that students can use their various strengths to help them learn – it is that which predominates in formal schooling. As such, we would be doing our pupils a disservice if we did not make it the primary mode of thought in the classroom.

One of the most powerful ways in which to help students develop this type of thinking is through modelling; namely the teacher's modelling of their own thought processes. Here is an example of what I mean:

Teacher: 'So, I'm looking at this source and I'm thinking to myself – how am I going to analyse it? Well, I might start by deciding what I want to get out of my analysis. Let's say that I want to find out what the source is saying, why it is saying it and how it compares to other sources that I know about. I can use these three aims to help me; I'll look at each one in turn as part of my analysis. Taking the first one then – what is the source saying – I am going to read through the source and note down the key points that I find. These will be the ones which indicate the big ideas or important information which the author is trying to get across...'

In the example, the teacher walks their students through the process of source analysis. In so doing, they are making explicit to their students what it is they expect them to do when they come to analyse a source. The teacher is providing pupils with a model which they can follow.

Such a method may be repeated with any aspect of thinking and at any level of schooling. The one prerequisite is that the teacher has paid sufficient attention to the processes of the mind in order to be able to talk about them in a way which is comprehensible. Given that this is a large part of the teacher's job, it is highly likely that this will always be the case.

How does it differentiate?

- Modelling thinking gives students an example to follow. This means it is easier for them to replicate the type of thinking which has been exemplified.
- By opening up thought processes and carefully describing them, the teacher is making plain that which might otherwise have been ambiguous. This makes it easier for students to engage with the work and to achieve success.
- Having a model to follow and being clear about exactly what the teacher is expecting (in terms of thinking) raises student confidence levels. This makes it more likely they will engage with the learning and make good progress.

23. Plan for VAK

What does it involve?

Students learn in different ways. One common analysis sees three broad categories defined: visual, audio and kinaesthetic (VAK). The argument goes that students are likely to have a preference for one of these approaches and therefore that is the way in which they learn best. The research base supporting this contention is limited and it would seem reductive to describe complex individuals as being a specific type of learner. With that said, the wider point – that students learn in different ways and that these include visual, audio and kinaesthetic approaches – remains valid.

We can take from this a differentiation technique which will prove useful: planning so as to incorporate the three main modes of learning in lessons or across a scheme of work. Using a mixture of strategies and activities means ensuring that different needs are catered for. More than that though, it ensures there is variety in lessons. This in itself aids engagement and increases motivation. Here are some suggested learning ideas for each of the categories:

- **Visual:** videos, images, pictures, cartoons, cartoon strips, dramatic performances, student presentations, slideshows, diagrams, flow-charts, graphs, hand-outs, anything containing the written word.
- **Audio:** videos, songs, speeches, sound recordings, discussion, debate, group work, pair work, lectures, talking heads, student presentations, oral explanations, interviews, conversations.
- **Kinaesthetic:** puzzles, drama, activities which involve movement, activities which involve handling or manipulating physical objects, card sorts, envoys, creating things, experiments, primary research.

A final point to note is that teaching is fundamentally about communication. The concept ought not to be restricted to one form or another. It is better to think about the range of ways in which ideas and information can be communicated (including indirectly, through the facilitation of learning). Such an approach is likely to lead the teacher to plan for VAK and therefore to differentiate for the pupils in their class.

How does it differentiate?

- All pupils learn in a variety of different ways. They may favour one method over another. Planning to include a range of elements in a lesson or scheme of work is a way of helping all learners to engage and to access the work.
- Variety helps to keep motivation and enthusiasm high. It adds novelty and surprise to lessons. This is good for all pupils.
- Providing a range of different learning opportunities also means providing a range of success opportunities. Students are sure to come across at least one activity or strategy which 'clicks' for them and helps them to make progress.
-

24. Data

What does it involve?

A great deal of data is collected on students as they pass through school. This includes information about performances in assessments, special educational needs, reading ages, cognitive ability and so on. In many schools this data is accessible through a specially-designed computer program. Here are five ways in which you might use data in order to differentiate:

- **When creating seating plans.** This is particularly apt if you do not know a class that well. You can use pupil data to help you decide who will sit where. For example, if it is indicated that a student has a specific need which requires significant support from the teacher if it is to be met, you might choose to place them near the front of the class to make it easier for you to access them.
- **When creating groups.** You might choose to develop groupings based on the student data you have in your possession. For example, it may be that you want a high-ability student in each group. Who these pupils are can be ascertained from a ranking of assessment results or cognitive ability test (CAT) scores.
- **When planning in general.** Again, this may prove to be particularly apt when you have little previous experience with a class (for example, the beginning of the year or when you take over a group mid-year). Using student data will help you to identify specific needs and give you an opportunity to plan how to meet these needs.
- **When developing specific elements of future lessons.** Elements are taken to include things such as questions, activities and end products (what you ask students to create). Data can help you to tailor these to the needs of your students. For example, you may note from your data that the class has an average reading age well below that which you would expect. This might lead

you to plan regular discussion activities in which you talk about short pieces of text relevant to the topic.

- **As a means to understand where students are at.** Student data is likely (though by no means certain) to give a reasonably accurate picture of where students are at in terms of their learning and the progress they have made to date. It can thus be used as a means to inform teaching and planning, allowing you to adapt your teaching to meet the needs of your pupils.

One final point to make about data: it is not the be all and end all. Data provides a snapshot, one which is usually but not always accurate. It is useful though ought not to be privileged over personal experience. You will get the richest, most useful information about your pupils through interacting with them. Data is a supplement or a precursor.

How does it differentiate?

- Data gives you information on students before you meet them. The downside of this is that it may cause you to view them without an open mind. The upside is that it allows you to plan to meet their needs from the word go.
- Data gives you an insight into the educational journey pupils have been on. This helps you to understand where they are at and to contextualise their present performance (and behaviour). Greater understanding is likely to lead to teaching which better meets pupils' needs.
- Data can be used to compare pupils. This means the teacher can pitch their teaching accordingly and can create groups based on relative abilities and skills.

25. Teaching Assistants

What does it involve?

Teaching assistants are those members of staff who support students both inside and outside of the classroom. Here are five ways in which you might direct them to work, so as to help you to differentiate:

- **Ask them to work with a specific student.** Some pupils have particularly acute needs and therefore will benefit from constant support during the course of a lesson. On another point, some students may find an aspect of the work very difficult. They would therefore benefit from short-term, focussed support from a teaching assistant (perhaps over the course of two lessons).
- **Ask them to work with a group of students.** You might put together a group of low-ability students and ask the teaching assistant to work with them, or you might do the same with a high-ability group. Either way, the teaching assistant will be able to give focussed support which is targeted to the specific needs of those pupils.
- **Ask them to deliver a part of the lesson.** While they are doing this, you could work intensively with a group of students who are behind or who are struggling to access the learning. This could be in a corner of the room, allowing you to keep an eye on the rest of the class and to intervene should the teaching assistant require any help.
- **Ask them to work with one or two students outside of the classroom.** It may be the case that one or two students are particularly disruptive, or that their needs are such that it is difficult for you or the teaching assistant to fully meet them in the classroom, in every single lesson. If this is so, you might ask the teaching assistant to work with these students in a different setting such as the school library.
- **Ask them to work with half the class.** If you identify two competing streams in your class, perhaps with one half of the

students making excellent progress while the other half struggle to keep up, you might like to split the group in two. The teaching assistant can then work with the more able half while you give your time to the rest of your students.

Three points to note regarding teaching assistants:

i. It is always preferable to speak to teaching assistants before the lesson. This means that you can indicate what you would like them to do and that you can also assess whether they feel comfortable with this.

ii. Some teaching assistants may work with certain students for a greater proportion of the week then you yourself do. If this is the case, ask them to tell you about that student – use their knowledge and experience to help you differentiate.

iii. Make sure that all your students give teaching assistants working in your class the same respect as they give you. Ensuring this happens will make everyone's life easier and result in more students making more progress.

How does it differentiate?

- Teaching assistants can give focussed support to specific students, helping them to make progress wherever they are at.
- Teaching assistants can take on work which frees the teacher up to support individual pupils or groups of pupils.
- Teaching assistants can use their experience and specialised knowledge to support the teacher and to help them differentiate for specific students.

Chapter Six - Words and Writing

In this chapter we look at twenty differentiation strategies, activities and techniques, all of which are connected to words and writing.

1. Keywords

What does it involve?

Language is central to learning. It is the means by which we convey our thoughts, feelings, beliefs and knowledge. Key words are those words which are of central importance to a subject or topic. Here are three methods by which to differentiate in relation to key words:

- **Provide students with a keyword glossary.** This could be given to all students, or just to those who need it most. It could be a ready-made sheet which has already been completed by the teacher, or it could contain some incomplete elements which pupils then have to fill in. Another alternative is to ask students to construct a glossary in the back of their books. They can add new words to this as time progresses – either at their own behest or on the teacher's instruction.
- **Provide students with a list of keywords and definitions appropriate to the lesson.** There will be some days when this is necessary, other days when it would be pointless. Examples of when it is likely to prove useful include: at the beginning of a unit of work, during the introduction to a topic, and in revision sessions. You might choose to hand such a list out to all students, or you might decide that it will only be appropriate for certain pupils.
- **Provide a list of keywords supplemented by examples of how these are used in sentences.** The advantage of such an approach is that it contextualises language and provides a model which students can follow – they can mimic or recreate

151

the examples in their own work. In addition, the examples will provide pupils with an extra opportunity to understand the meaning of the keywords (they will be coming to terms with them in context, rather than in the more abstract manner involve in learning definitions).

How does it differentiate?

- Giving students extra support in understanding keywords will help them to access the higher-order learning which takes place in the lesson. Pupils will be better placed to follow what is going on and to process ideas and information if they first have a grasp of the language of the topic.
- Demonstrating how keywords are used in sentences helps students to understand their meaning and purpose. If pupils can grasp this, they will be better placed to make progress with the work.
- Students who are less able in a subject often have lower literacy levels than their peers. Providing them with extra support linked to understanding and using keywords will go some way toward bridging this gap.

2. Simple Language

What does it involve?

The more complex the language you use, the less likely it is that all the students in your class will be able to access the meaning. Differentiate by simplifying your language.

Consider the different places you might do this:

- When speaking to the whole class.
- When speaking to individuals
- When writing comments.

- On PowerPoint or IWB slides.
- On hand-outs.

Simplifying does not mean dumbing down. It means making things clear and easy to understand. Here is an example, taken from Sociology:

'Primary socialisation is the process by which individuals are taught the norms, values, rules and roles of society within the family unit. It is an on-going process which begins at birth and is joined by secondary socialisation – that is, the influence of other agents such as the media, peer groups and schooling – as the child grows older.'

There are a number of ways in which we might simplify this, including:

- We could use less technical vocabulary and less subject-specific terminology.
- We could explain the terminology more clearly as we go along.
- We could use a different sentence structure.
- We could give simple examples.
- We could relate it to students' personal experience.

Here is an example of how the same meaning could be conveyed more simply:

'When a baby is born, their parents teach them many things. This includes lots that we take for granted. For example: how to talk, how to use the toilet, how to eat at a table using cutlery and so on. This process goes on for many years and is called primary socialisation. Primary means first and socialisation means being made a part of society. If we are socialised, then we fit into what society thinks is normal. As we get older, other things influence us. These include education, the media and our peer groups. We call the process through which they teach and affect us secondary socialisation. This is because it comes second and because it also involves being made a part of society.'

In this rewrite I have followed the second and third points made above. Sentences are kept shorter, meaning they are easier to follow, and keywords are explained as they come up. Despite these changes, the meaning which the text conveys is similar, if not identical, to that of the more complex original.

How does it differentiate?

- Using simple language helps all students to access the meaning of what you are saying.
- Simple language does not mean dumbing down, it means communicating clearly. Communicating clearly means more students will be able to access the meaning of what the teacher says. If this is the case, it is likely that more pupils in the class will have their thinking stretched. This is because you can only be challenged if you are able to at least get a foothold in as a starting point. If this is not the case, then the task is impossible rather than just plain difficult.
- If students can understand the meaning of what the teacher is communicating then they will be more likely to make progress, regardless of their starting point.

3. Keyword Display

What does it involve?

Display keywords around the room. This will help students to use those words, to learn their meanings and to memorise them. Here are five ways in which you might do this:

- **Washing Line.** Hang a piece of string such that it runs from one side of your classroom to the other. Buy some clothes pegs and laminate sheets of paper with keywords written on them. Attach the sheets to the washing line using the clothes pegs. You might like to invite students to put new words on the washing line – this could be a reward or could form part of a game (with pupils having to correctly explain the meaning of a word before they are allowed to attach it to the washing line).

- **Display Board.** Fill a display board with keywords which are common to your subject, to the topic you are studying, or which form an important part of general writing (for example, connectives such as 'and', 'however' and 'therefore'). If you have multiple display boards, you might like to have a different category of keywords on each one. If you do not have display boards, pieces of paper with keywords printed onto them could be stuck to the wall. A display area can be formed by making a border of coloured paper around the keywords.

- **Words and Definitions.** Create a display which consists of keywords next to their definitions. This will be akin to a glossary set out on your classroom wall. You might like to supplement the definitions with appropriate images. This will further help students to access the meaning of the keywords.

- **Keyword Create.** Plan a task in which you and your class create the keyword display together. You could do this at the beginning of a topic as a way of introducing students to some or all of the key vocabulary they will need to learn over the forthcoming weeks. Divide students into groups and give each group a selection of (related) keywords for which they have to create a display segment. You might like to provide success criteria such as: include an image, make sure all definitions are clear, and create keywords which are eye-catching. This will help to structure the task and ensure a degree of uniformity across the final display as a whole.

- **On-going Display.** Create an empty display area in your classroom. Explain to students that, as the topic progresses, you and they will be developing the display until it is complete. This will involve one of two things. On the one hand, you might choose to devote a little section of each lesson to display work, with all students in the class making keyword posters based on the words which they have learnt. On the other hand, you might like to select a different group each lesson to create the keyword posters. In this second case, the idea is that, by the end of the topic, all members of the class will have contributed to the creation of the display.

How does it differentiate?

- Displaying keywords around the room helps students to learn, memorise and use these terms.
- Displaying keywords around the room means that pupils have prompts available which can help them if they get stuck.
- Having students take part in the creation of keyword displays is a good way to get them thinking about and engaging with key terms. The activities mentioned above are concrete and easy to access. This means that all pupils will have the opportunity of contextualising and understanding abstract significations which, in other settings, might prove more difficult to come to terms with.

4.   Keyword Discussion

What does it involve?

Use discussion activities as a means to help students come to terms with keywords. Here are five ways in which to do this:

- **Paired Discussion.** Introduce pupils to one or more new words. Explain the meaning of the words and give examples of their use. Having done this, invite pupils to discuss the keywords in pairs and to come up with three sentences which demonstrate their correct use. Encourage students to practise and refine these sentences in their pairs. Finally, draw the whole class back together and ask different groups to share their sentences. These should be checked for accuracy by the whole class, in a teacher-led discussion.

- **Group Discussion.** Divide students into groups of three. Give each group a hand-out containing the keywords you wish to introduce, definitions of these terms and examples of their use. Display the following series of questions on the board: Have you come across the word before and if so, where? Why might this word be particularly useful? In what circumstances might this word be used and who would use it? What does the example tell you about the meaning of the word? Can you give a further example of how to use the word in a sentence or a paragraph? Invite groups to work through the keywords, answering the series of questions for each individual case. You might like to choose a member of each group to be a scribe. They would then write down the answers to the questions which their group members come up with. The activity could be concluded with a whole-class discussion, brief presentations from a select number of groups or through the use of envoys to share answers.
- **Research Discussion.** Divide the class into groups. Assign a keyword to each group. Explain that the aim of the activity is for groups to research the keyword and to be ready to present their findings to the rest of the class. Provide various research materials, such as encyclopaedias, dictionaries, thesauri, internet access and textbooks, for pupils to use. You might also like to display a set of success criteria or a series of questions on the board – either of which could be used by students to structure their work and their final presentations.
- **Whole-Class Discussion.** Introduce the class to one or more keywords. Ask whether anyone has come across the words before. If some students have, take this as an opportunity to begin a discussion about their meaning and use. Otherwise, explain the meaning and use of the words, including by giving examples, and then begin a discussion through questions such as those indicated in the 'group discussion' point above.
- **Drama Discussion.** Divide the class into groups. Give each group a keyword (this could be different for each group, the same for

everybody or a small number which are repeated) and ask them to create a dramatic presentation of that keyword. After sufficient time has passed, invite various groups to come up to the front and showcase their performances. If students struggle to conceive of how they might dramatize their keyword, provide them with a list of options such as the following: Create a role-play showing someone using the keyword in real life; Create a role-play showing the keyword in the world (perhaps happening to, influencing or affecting people); Create a freeze-frame showing your keyword and its relationship to a group of people; Create a physical model of your keyword; Create a role-play based around a conflict to do with your keyword.

How does it differentiate?

- Talking about things is an effective prelude to writing about them. Using discussion to introduce keywords will help students to use them in their written work.
- Discussion is accessible to all. Speech comes before writing and most pupils are likely to be more skilled in the former than in the latter. Therefore, using discussion is a way of playing to the whole class's strengths in order to help them make progress (including in subsequent written work).
- Speech is instantly editable and mistakes are not recorded. It is therefore a good medium through which to engage with new ideas and concepts. Students will be less likely to experience failure or frustration in their early encounters with keywords. This means they will be more motivated, more engaged with the topic and more likely to make progress.

5.   Keyword Context

What does it involve?

Providing context to keywords gives students something to grab hold of, allowing them to situate the terms within a wider framework. Here are five ways in which you might provide such opportunities:

- **Give Examples.** As has been noted elsewhere, examples give specific cases which provide evidence, proof and demonstration to abstract or general statements. When explaining keywords to students, examples will help them to contextualise the new terms. It is a way of indicating that the meaning of a keyword is shown through a certain thing. By extension, this means that the meaning is not shown through a whole range of other things. It is like sticking a pin in a map – you are signalling the place through the point of the pin, but you are also signalling that everywhere else is not what you are interested in.
- **Pupils' Prior Experience.** Imagine a pupil knows X, Y and Z. You introduce new thing A to them. They have never heard of it and, as far as they are aware, do not have any experience of it. Therefore, if they are to assimilate and understand it, they will need to do so in a way which is abstract and purely mental. Imagine now that you show them (or facilitate their finding out) that A connects to X. Suddenly, the new information makes more sense to the student – they are able to fit it into their existing understanding and the conceptual framework on which their thinking depends. This is the benefit of using pupils' prior experience as a means to contextualise keywords.
- **Use of Media.** Another way in which to provide some context to keywords is through the use of media. This could involve a video which demonstrates a term, a talking head in which an expert speaks about the meaning or use of a term or a sound clip in which the term is used in conversation.
- **Narrative.** We have considered the use and relevance of narrative elsewhere. Regarding keywords, it is a good way of

providing context and can be called upon in three distinct forms. First, the teacher can tell students a story in which one or more keywords are exemplified, used or made plain. Second, a piece of media can be used which tells a story centring on the keyword. Third, a story written about an individual (such as from a newspaper or magazine), and in which one or more keywords feature or are relevant, can be read, analysed and explored by students and the teacher.

- **Case Studies.** These provide concrete, real-world demonstrations of keywords in action. For example, in a geography lesson the teacher might introduce pupils to erosion, as well as to other associated key terms. This would be followed up through the use of a case study concerned with the gradual erosion of a coastal area in which people live. Such an example would provide graphic, and possibly emotional, contextualisation of the key terms – making it easy for students to understand them and, subsequently, to use them.

How does it differentiate?

- Contextualising keywords gives students something concrete to grab hold of. This makes new terms more accessible as not all students will find processing abstract information straightforward.
- All of the methods outlined above give students something which is memorable – a multimedia experience or a story for example. These act as aids to recollection, making it easier for students to store and recall key terms. This is an area which less able students often find difficult.
- Contextualising keywords combines abstract (linguistic) and concrete (the context) thinking. This helps all students in the class to make progress and to develop their understanding of the topic on both levels of thought.

6. Antonyms

What does it involve?

Antonyms are opposites:

An antonym of big is small.

An antonym of white is black.

An antonym of fast is slow.

When you introduce students to new words, talk to them about the antonyms of these words. This will help pupils to understand the meaning of the new terms. It will make it clear what the words do not mean (and therefore what it is they do mean). If possible, use simple antonyms with which students will already be familiar.

Here is a logical explanation of how antonyms can help pupils understand new words. Imagine that a student knows X, Y and Z. You introduce them to new thing A. Your introduction involves stating the word which signifies A, explaining the meaning of this word and then giving examples. In so doing, you have started to create some connections and context around A. Next, you give a simple antonym to A. Let us say that the student is already familiar with the antonym. In fact, it turns out that the antonym is X. Immediately the pupil is in a position to connect A to that which they already know. In so doing, they are identifying a relationship between A and X, they are incorporating A into their existing knowledge and understanding and they are creating relationships between A and Y and Z (A is an antonym of X, therefore it is not an antonym of Y or Z).

From this example we can see that the provision of an antonym – one with which, as a word, students are already familiar – can help pupils to learn the meanings of new terms.

Here are five ways in which you might want to introduce antonyms:

- Introduce your class to one or more key terms. Explain and exemplify these and then provide some appropriate antonyms.
- Give students a hand-out which contains a set of keywords appropriate to the topic complete with definitions and antonyms.
- Give students a list of keywords and ask them to find out the antonyms of these (you might like to use 'opposites' as a non-technical term). Some dictionaries contain antonyms, including some word processing dictionaries. The internet is also a good resource students can use to complete this task.
- Give students two lists: one of keywords and one of antonyms. They look up the meanings of the keywords using dictionaries and then match each keyword to the correct antonym.
- Display a keyword on the board next to three possible antonyms. Explain what the keyword means and then ask students to work out which is the correct antonym. This task could also be done in groups, with students receiving a hand-out containing a series of keywords next to definitions and multiple possible antonyms.

How does it differentiate?

- Antonyms help students to understand words with which they are not familiar. Using simple antonyms means calling on what pupils already know. This is a way of helping all pupils to access the learning.
- Antonyms provide an alternative path to understanding (or a supplementary path) compared to examples and explanations. They therefore offer another way of engaging students and of helping them to access the learning. Some pupils may find this path easier.
- Antonyms provide scaffolding which takes students some of the way towards a sound understanding of a word. They can therefore be used to help all pupils make progress.

7. Dictionary Champions

What does it involve?

Appoint members of your class as 'dictionary champions'. The specific requirements of this role are flexible and may include any of the following:

- Looking up the meanings of new words which come up during whole-class discussions or periods of teacher talk and communicating these to the rest of the group.
- Creating a glossary of new words during the course of a lesson or series of lessons, with the teacher then photocopying this so that all students can have a copy.
- Looking up the meanings of words on behalf of the group with which the student is working. In this instance, the teacher will need to appoint a dictionary champion for each group (and provide a similar number of dictionaries).
- Finding out words relevant to the topic that have not come up during the course of the lesson, obtaining the definitions of these, and then sharing them with the rest of the class. A variation on this involves the teacher giving the dictionary champions a list of extra words at the beginning of the lesson and then asking them to present the meanings of these towards the end of the session.
- Looking up the meaning of words which come from a specific source, for example a video, a talk given by a speaker or a newspaper article. In this context, the dictionary champions will be working in real-time for the rest of the class, helping them to better understand the source as they go along.

It is good to rotate the role so as to give a number of students an opportunity. In addition, you might like to vary the requirements depending on who the champions are at any particular time. The fourth point, for example, may be better suited to more able students, whereas the third point would be appropriate for all pupils.

How does it differentiate?

- Dictionary champions can teach their peers the meaning of the words they look up. This creates a different teacher-student relationship in the class; pupils are taught by their contemporaries, with whom they share codes, experiences and conceptual frameworks. This can make it easier for students to access the learning.
- Making more able students dictionary champions provides an opportunity to challenge them and stretch their thinking – as in the fourth point outlined above.
- Encouraging – even lionising – the use of dictionaries is a great way of getting students to see them as tools which can help them with their work. If pupils do come to see dictionaries in this way then they will have a constant companion which can aid them in making progress at all times.

8. Structure Guidelines

What does it involve?

Structure guidelines are about two things: minimising ambiguity and allowing students to focus on the detail of what they are doing. They entail any means by which the teacher provides students with a framework for the work which has been set. Here are three examples:

- In an essay task, the teacher might provide students with guidelines indicating what should be contained in each paragraph. For example: Paragraph one = Introduction; Paragraphs two and three = arguments for the statement; Paragraphs four and five = arguments against the statement; Paragraph six = Conclusion.
- In a presentation task, the teacher might provide guidelines indicating what should be covered and in what order. For example: Begin by outlining what you will talk about, then make

your first key point and support this with examples. Repeat this for your second and third points. Then provide some time in which the audience can ask questions. Finally, sum up your presentation.

- In a primary research task, the teacher might provide pupils with guidelines covering how to report their findings. For example: You will need to create a report which contains the following: Introduction; Hypothesis; Aims; Rationale; Background Research; Methodology; Results; Analysis; Evaluation.

In each of these cases, the guidelines make clear to pupils what their finished work should look like, in terms of its layout and structure.

Structure guidelines minimise ambiguity by providing a reference point for what it is the teacher is asking students to do. It may be the case that the word 'essay' or 'presentation' does not have the same connotations for students as it does for the teacher. By providing clear guidance the teacher is sidestepping this possibility (and the potential problems which might emanate from it). In addition, even if students have a general idea of what a specific task ought to involve, they may still struggle to articulate this analytically – that is, in a manner which involves separate elements being identified and then put together into a sequence. For both these reasons, structure guidelines make it easier for pupils to succeed in a task.

A second point to note is that all creation – whatever its nature – involves both form and content. The provision of structure guidelines is essentially a provision of form. It allows students to fully focus their attention on matters of content. And it is this that is the basis of most learning in most lessons. However, with that said, it can also be noted that through the manipulation of content in accordance with a given form, students will come to better understand that form – they will be learning it through practise, just as they are learning the content through application, analysis, synthesis and evaluation. Therefore, structure guidelines actually aid rather than sacrifice the learning of skills despite their giving primacy to content.

How does it differentiate?

- Structure guidelines minimise ambiguity. This makes it easier for students to achieve success. This is because they know precisely what it is that the teacher wants them to do.
- Structure guidelines allow students to focus on content. This makes it easier for them to achieve success because their minds will not be split between competing demands.
- All students will be able to produce work to their own highest standard using structure guidelines. Therefore the technique helps pupils to make progress regardless of their starting position.

9. Sentence Starters

What does it involve?

Sentence starters are just that – the starts of sentences. Here are some examples:

- In my opinion...
- The first thing that I think is...
- Many people would argue...
- Today I have...
- The one which I think is best is...

In each case, the teacher is providing students with a little leg up; a means to get started; a route into the work.

Beginning a piece of writing can be difficult for students. They may not know how to start; they may know a number of different ways but be uncertain of which to choose; they may not want to start; they may have a fear of failure which manifests itself as a belief that however they choose to start will be wrong; or they may be put off by the whole act of writing. Sentence starters get past all these issues in a moment. They can be used in an ad hoc manner, but here are five specific approaches you might take as well:

- **General Sentence Starters.** Provide sentence starters for the whole class. These could be displayed on the board or, if you are only using one, spoken aloud for students to then write down.
- **Specific Sentence Starters.** Provide sentence starters to specific students who struggle to begin their writing. These could be given out on a printed sheet or the teacher could see each pupil individually and speak the sentence starters to them in turn.
- **Structure Guideline Sentence Starters.** Provide sentence starters for each part of the overall structure of the work. This helps students to get started, to break their work up into sections and to begin each of those sections in a focussed way.
- **Student-led Sentence Starters.** Having explained a task, ask students to work in pairs to come up with some appropriate sentence starters. These are then shared in a brief whole-class discussion, with the best being written down on the board for all to see.
- **Student Example Sentence Starters.** Having explained the task and set students off, allow a minute or two to pass and then ask for volunteers to read their opening sentences. Pupils who are struggling to begin can either copy what they hear or use it as inspiration for their own opening sentences.

How does it differentiate?

- Sentence starters provide students who might struggle to get started on writing tasks a means to get going.
- Sentence starters are a way of shepherding students into a task, thus allowing them to focus on the content of their writing.
- Sentence starters offer students a model of how to begin their work. It is likely that over time pupils will internalise this. In

turn, this will help them to become better writers who possess the confidence to get started on their own.

10. Writing Frame

What does it involve?

A writing frame provides students with a guide as to what they are to write and how they are to write it. The degree of detail can vary but what will remain common is a framework directing students in their work. In terms of design, a writing frame will usually consist of a piece of paper on which instructions of some kind are printed or written. This description is necessarily vague because writing frames can take many forms. Here are five examples which demonstrate the approach:

- **Genre Writing Frames.** By genre we do not mean types of fiction writing but types of writing full stop. Genres that are common in school include essays, stories, reports, newspaper articles and reviews. In all these cases there are rules governing how the piece of work should be constructed. A genre writing frame provides students with guidance on the specific form of writing they are doing. For example, an essay writing frame might include instructions covering indicative content and appropriate sentence starters for each paragraph.
- **Sentence Starter Writing Frames.** These involve pupils being given a piece of paper on which there are a series of sentence starters. Each of these signals a new element in the overall piece of prose pupils are aiming to construct. Such an approach is most useful when students have severe difficulties with extended writing or when they are at an early stage of language development (either within the traditional framework of schooling or because they are learning English as an additional language).

- **Content Specific Writing Frames.** These concentrate on the specific content pupils are expected to include in each part of their work. This may be at section level, at paragraph level or, in certain cases, at sentence level. For example, if the teacher set students the task of creating a report on parrots, they might provide a frame such as the following: Introduction – explain what parrots are, where they live and what the main species are; Section One – choose one species and explain in detail how that species looks, lives and interacts with other birds; Section Two – explain the impact that humans are having on the natural habitat of parrots in one area of the world; Section Three – evaluate the arguments for and against increasing government intervention to protect parrots in the wild; Conclusion – sum up your findings about parrots.
- **Improvement Writing Frames.** Identify an area which an individual student, a group of students or the whole class could improve. Create a writing frame which will help them to make the appropriate changes in their work. For example, if your students are failing to support the points they make with evidence, you might create a paragraph by paragraph writing frame focussing on the issue. This could begin with specific examples which students mimic, then move onto suggestions of where suitable evidence might be found and finally finish by asking pupils to identify appropriate evidence on their own.
- **Mark Scheme Based Writing Frames.** Construct a series of writing frames linked to what students need to do in order to achieve various levels on a mark scheme. Pupils can then choose the writing frame which they feel most closely matches their abilities. They can also cherry-pick elements from other writing frames, if they so wish.

How does it differentiate?

- Writing frames leave students free to concentrate on the act of writing and the myriad decisions which need to be taken regarding content and grammar. This makes the task easier, allowing more students to engage successfully with the work and to experience success.
- Writing frames can provide less able students with a leg-up, helping to boost their confidence by making starting and sustaining a piece of writing easier and more accessible.
- Writing frames can be targeted to specific students, used as a means to help all pupils to improve and made to be challenging.

11. Planning Pro-Forma

What does it involve?

A planning pro-forma is a document you hand out to students and which they use to help plan their work. It is a blank form which serves as a model. All students use the same version, tailoring the contents to suit their needs.

Here are three ways in which you might use planning pro-formas:

- Create separate pro-formas for different types of writing, for example, essays, stories and reports. These can be used repeatedly throughout a course of study. An advantage of this approach is that students will internalise the questions or divisions which go to make up the pro-formas. This means that in the future they will be able to plan their work without needing any assistance.
- Create highly detailed pro-formas for less able students. These should contain a series of questions or divisions which break the piece of work up into manageable sections. At each point you might like to provide pupils with a range of options from which

they can choose. This is a further way of supporting students who struggle to plan extended pieces of writing.

- Create challenging pro-formas for your most able students. These could contain taxing questions which cause pupils to think more deeply about their work, both in terms of form and in terms of content.

How does it differentiate?

- A pro-forma will help a student to plan their work. This means that they will be more likely to make progress and produce something which meets the teacher's success criteria.
- The plan pupils produce will help them to sustain their writing – something which many students might otherwise find difficult.
- The teacher can construct pro-formas which are targeted to the needs of their pupils, helping all in the class to make progress, regardless of their starting position.

12. Scrap Paper

What does it involve?

Scrap paper is a thinking tool. It is an extension of the mind; something which humans can use to expand their capabilities. For example, if you want to remember a phone number, you may well choose to write it down on a scrap of paper which you then store somewhere for safe keeping. You will have done this because you know that it is a much easier and more reliable method than trying to memorise the number.

Here is another example. A friend asks you to help them with some accounting. They have a collection of receipts, the prices of which they need to add up. They call out the numbers to you one by one. It is you job to produce a running total. After the first five receipts have been read out you ask your friend to stop and go back to the start. You take a piece of scrap paper and write down each price in turn, perhaps labelling them '1,2,3,4...' When the last price has been called out you add up the collection of figures. In so doing, you make further notes on the scrap paper – what we would commonly call the 'working out' involved in a mathematical operation. Finally, you present your friend with the total and the scrap paper. They can check your calculations if they so wish.

And finally, a third example. You are sat in an examination hall. Two hours stretch out in front of you. The question paper is deposited on your desk. There are eight questions of which you must choose two to answer. You will need to spend an hour on each. At the book of your answer booklet there are some blank pages. You turn to these and make a rough plan of what each of your essays will contain. Throughout the examination you refer to this, using it as a guide and point of reference. With the plans sketched out and recorded you can give all your energies to writing what it is you want to write.

Encourage students to use scrap paper and you will be encouraging them to use a thinking tool which can extend the capacity of their minds. In particular, you will be giving them a means of circumventing the limitations of their short-term memory. This will help them to learn, to think and to make good progress in your lessons. Here are five specific examples of how scrap paper might be used:

- To plan something.
- To record information.
- For working something out.
- To test an idea.
- To organise one's thoughts.

Here are five ways you might physically include scrap paper in your classroom:

- Give every student an exercise book which they use as scrap paper.

- Have a drawer of scrap paper which pupils can access as they wish.
- Place a basket of scrap paper on each table.
- Encourage students to use the backs of their exercise books as a scrap paper section.
- Give students mini-whiteboards and marker pens. These are akin to scrap paper.

How does it differentiate?

- Scrap paper helps students to overcome the limitations of their short-term memory. It therefore expands what they are capable of, helping them to make progress.
- Scrap paper is a tool students can use to help them with their learning. It is probable that pupils who are less able will benefit the most because they are the ones who are more likely to struggle with complex cognitive operations.
- Wherever a student is at, scrap paper can be a great help. A pupil doing advanced calculus can expand their mind through its use in the same way that a pupil doing simple multiplication can.

13. Bullet Points and Tables

What does it involve?

Bullet points and tables are thinking tools, albeit ones which function in a different way to scrap paper. Each offers a means by which to present information. Two examples will demonstrate the potential utility of these particular approaches:

Example One: I like chocolate and pizza and lollipops but the thing I like most of all is chocolate biscuits, especially the ones which have chocolate chips in them. I also like going on holiday to places which are far away and which have lots of sunshine. This is because I like the sun and I like playing outdoors with my friends.

Things I like:

- Chocolate
- Chocolate Biscuits
- Pizza
- Lollipops
- Going on Holiday
- Sunshine
- Playing Outdoors
- Playing with Friends

Example Two: Many people would argue that the voting age should be lowered to sixteen; not least because of the other rights people of that age have, such as being allowed to marry and being allowed to join the army. On the other hand, it has been argued that at sixteen years of age young people are still developing and do not have the maturity or life experience to participate fully in democracy. At the same time, many have countered that this is true of plenty of adults and therefore is not a valid argument in relation to age.

Arguments for and against lowering the voting age to sixteen:

Arguments For	Arguments Against
Sixteen year-olds can marry and join the army.	Sixteen year-olds are still in a developmental stage – physically, mentally and emotionally.
Sixteen year-olds have other rights therefore they should have the right to vote.	Sixteen year-olds are not mature enough to vote sensibly.
Plenty of adults are not mature or do not have life experience therefore why shouldn't sixteen year-olds also be given the vote?	Sixteen year-olds do not have the necessary life experience to take full part in democracy.

In both cases, information presented in prose has been transformed. In example one, a list of bullet points has been constructed. This contains only the specific pieces of information relevant to the subject. It is therefore easier to assimilate and manipulate. In example two, a table has been constructed which delineates the arguments for and against the proposition. Each argument is established as a separate piece of information belonging to one of the two categories. Again, this makes the information easier to assimilate and manipulate.

You can use bullet points and tables in the following ways in order to help the students you teach:

- Where you believe it will be of benefit, display information in bullet points or tables.
- Encourage students to use bullet points or tables when they are analysing a text or other type of source.
- Encourage students to use bullet points and tables in their planning. This will help them to identify and order the information they wish to include in their work.
- Demonstrate how bullet points or tables can be used as a transition stage between analysis and synthesis. This involves creating one of the two based on an examination of an item and then using what one has created to craft a piece of work which is one's own.
- Scaffold tasks by creating a bullet point list or table of information through a whole-class discussion. Students can then use this as they complete their work individually.

One final point: Bullet points and tables are a means of displaying and conveying information simply and clearly. They are not a panacea and inevitably some things are lost through their use as compared to other forms of communication (this is the case with any form of analysis). Students should see them as a tool or an aid which can help them en route to their main goal – the creation of an extended piece of work.

How does it differentiate?

- Bullet points and tables display information clearly and simply. This means that more students in the class can access and use that information.
- Students can use bullet points and tables in their own planning. It will help them to clarify their thinking and to bridge the gap between analysis and synthesis.
- The teacher can provide less able students with bullet points and tables which they have created. This means that some of the analytical work will have been done for them, making the task easier and more accessible.

14. Individual Writing

What does it involve?

This incorporates all those tasks in which students are expected to produce a piece of writing while working on their own. It refers to extended pieces rather than small or sequential items – such as might be produced in response to a series of questions. Here are some examples of individual writing tasks:

- Writing an essay
- Creating a report
- Writing up something which the student has done (such as an experiment or an investigation)
- Writing a story
- Writing a personal response to a piece of stimulus material

In each case, pupils are being asked to construct something which is a reflection of their own understanding. Therefore, differentiation is inherent in the task. The process of translating that which is in one's mind into the written word is a process which will be pitched at whatever level the student is at – in terms of their own understanding, their ability to introspect and their skill in manipulating the written word.

In addition, there is scope within any piece of extended individual writing for students to make choices and decisions based on what they think and what they believe themselves to be capable of. As an example of this, consider a time when you have marked a set of books containing such work. It is highly likely that you will have come across a wide range of responses –in terms of content, style and, possibly, form.

A final point to note is that individual writing tasks, if they give students sufficient freedom, provide an outlet for self-expression. This term should not be restrained to creative writing. Analytical and evaluative self-expression is equally important and just as fulfilling. In any case, pupils will be motivated by the thought of being able to share what they think with the teacher; at being able to engage in productive, creative work – the manifestation of what is inside them (thoughts, feelings, ideas and so on) such that it can be understood and affirmed by others.

How does it differentiate?

- Individual writing tasks give students freedom to explore their ideas. This freedom results in pupils making choices and decisions about the work they create and therefore differentiating on their own initiative.
- Individual writing is challenging for all students as it represents a coming together of various skills and knowledge at the highest level of which the pupil is capable.
- Individual writing, when carefully structured and supported, motivates students by providing them with an opportunity to be productive and creative. It also allows students to communicate that which they think, feel and believe – something which most of us want to do as part of daily lives, especially when we are engaged in learning.

15. Images

What does it involve?

Teachers can use images throughout their lessons in order to help students understand the meaning of words. Here are five examples of what this might entail:

- **Images on PowerPoint or IWB Slides.** Many teachers use Microsoft PowerPoint or an interactive whiteboard programme to plan their lessons. They then use the slides they create as the basis for their teaching. A wonderful benefit of this approach is the incredible ease with which you can copy images from the internet and paste them into the documents you create. Taking advantage of this leads to presentations in which words are supplemented by images. This in turn helps students to decode and memorise meaning.
- **Images on Worksheets.** Including images on worksheets gives students a different medium through which to learn as well as a supplement which helps them to decode the meaning of words, sentences and paragraphs. Images can also provide examples or contextualisation or that which is written. For example, a worksheet introducing a new concept – one which students are unlikely to have encountered before – will be much more accessible if it contains appropriate images as well as text.
- **Images of Keywords.** This chapter has noted the importance of keywords and there are a number of entries focussed on this element of teaching. Another way in which to help students learn the meaning of keywords – as well as their correct use – is to accompany them with images. In so doing, you will be providing a visual definition, an exemplification and a contextualisation of the terms.
- **Images for Specific Students.** It may be the case that specific pupils in your class will benefit from the provision of worksheets or hand-outs which contain a series of images linked to the words written on these documents. This might include students

who have lower levels of literacy or who are learning English as an additional language.

- **Other Types of Images.** These include diagrams, flow-charts, cartoon strips and symbols (among others). All of these convey information in different ways. All can be kept in mind as useful tools which the teacher might call upon in order to communicate meaning or aid students in developing their understanding.

How does it differentiate?

- Images can be used as a supplement to words. This means that students have a further opportunity to access the meaning of those words – one which is simpler and less abstract.
- Images can provide an exemplification, illustration or contextualisation of what a word means. In each case, students are not solely reliant on situating a word within an abstract system (language). Instead, they can connect it to their existing knowledge and experience as well.
- Images are a great help to students whose literacy levels are behind those of their peers for whatever reason. If a teacher makes an effort to use them throughout their lessons, they will be making an effort to help these pupils engage with the learning and, subsequently, to make progress.

16. Talk Then Write

What does it involve?

Preceding writing tasks with discussion is of great benefit to all students. It gives an opportunity for pupils to order their thoughts, articulate these and then refine them. The medium allows instant editing and immediate responses. In addition, it is ephemeral – meaning that mistakes are not visible after the event. A further point to add is that speaking is not a technology in the same way that writing is. While it has to be learnt and varying degrees of sophistication are evident in any random selection of the population, the fact is that it is an integral part of human beings rather than an extension – as writing is.

All this means that preceding writing with talking is a way of scaffolding the former process. Pupils are able to do some of the work which writing requires (ordering information, articulating what that which one thinks, refining this so as to make it clearer, choosing the correct words and so on) in a medium with which they are extremely familiar and in which they are, most likely, highly skilled.

Here are ten ways in which you might help students to talk before they write:

- Free discussion in pairs.
- Free discussion in groups.
- Discussion in pairs or groups around one or more questions set by the teacher.
- Discussion in pairs in which students take it in turns to present their ideas to each other.
- Discussion in pairs or groups based around some stimulus material.
- Students work in pairs and take it in turns to interview one another about their ideas.
- Students walk around the classroom and find three peers to discuss their ideas with, one after the other.
- Students work in pairs and share their ideas. Groups of four are then formed, with pupils explaining the ideas of their partner to the new members.
- Students work in groups of three or four. Each pupil is given thirty seconds to advocate for their ideas. There then follows a minute of questioning. The process is repeated until everyone has had their turn.
- The class is split in half. Students sit in two rows, facing one another. The pairings which are formed have two minutes to discuss their ideas. When the time is up, one row of pupils

stands up. They move along one seat in order to create new pairings. A new discussion takes place. The process is repeated a third time before the activity ends.

How does it differentiate?

- During discussion, students will be able to order, articulate and refine their thoughts. This will make writing easier for them. By the time they begin they will have already made significant progress and will be able to concentrate their attentions on the act of writing itself.
- Discussion is more accessible to students than writing. Using the former as a precursor to the latter is a way of drawing all pupils in and helping them to access that which they might find difficult.
- Generally, students like to talk. Using discussion is thus a way of motivating and engaging pupils.

17. Create-a-Glossary

What does it involve?

A glossary is an index of keywords complete with definitions. Here are five ways to get your students to create their own glossaries:

- At the beginning of a topic, give students a hand-out which contains all the keywords which they will encounter over the forthcoming weeks. During the course of the period of study, pupils can complete their glossary by writing in the definitions they learn. You might like to leave enough space between keywords for students to write examples of the keywords being used in sentences as well. A systematic approach to this particular method involves setting aside a short amount of time at the end of every lesson for pupils to define and exemplify the keywords they have learnt in the session.

- During a course of study, or even across the entire year, ask students to write down keywords and their definitions in the backs of their books, as they come across them.
- Choose two or three pupils as 'Glossary Champions'. Their job is to create a glossary entry for each keyword that comes up and to stick this on the classroom wall in a section designated as the glossary display. Pupils can refer to this area during the course of their studies.
- If your room is set up such that students sit in groups, designate a glossary champion at each table. Their job is to add any keywords to a group glossary which is kept in the middle of the desks, such that each member of the group can access it as and when they wish. Rotate glossary champions over a few lessons so that everyone has an opportunity to take on the role.
- At the beginning of a topic, put students into groups and supply each group with a selection of relevant material (such as handouts, textbooks, worksheets and so on). Invite the groups to search through the material in order to find as many keywords (and their definitions) as possible. These should be collated in a glossary which pupils can then use through the forthcoming lessons.

How does it differentiate?

- Students can use glossaries to check the meaning of words. They therefore act as an aid to students, both in terms of helping them to remember key terms and in helping them to get to grips with the meanings of these words.
- If a student finds themselves stuck, they can turn to a glossary for help. Using glossaries is therefore a way in which pupils can help themselves to be independent.
- The construction of a glossary involves pupils manipulating and engaging with keywords, definitions and, in some cases, examples. All pupils will make progress through such a process.

18. Point Out the Word

What does it involve?

An ostensive definition involves explaining the meaning of a word by pointing out examples. So, you and I might be walking down the road when you ask me: 'What is this colour 'red'?' Clearly it would be difficult for me to articulate the meaning of the word red; it is likely that I would have to resort to giving examples of things which are red, making comparisons between red and other colours, or indicating which words and images red often connotes (for example, blushing). None of this would really be satisfactory. What if you came from an area in which fire engines and post-boxes were blue? What if you were unfamiliar with other colours as well? And how accurate is it to explain the colour red by resorting to those things which it connotes?

The best way in which I could answer your question is by pointing out examples of what red means. Let us imagine that, as we continued walking down the road, a ladybird flew past, then a can of Coca-Cola appeared and, finally, we came across a traffic light stuck on 'stop'. In each case I could have pointed to the item and said to you: 'There – that is red.'

Ostensive definitions are an extra tool teachers can call on in their quest to make things clear for students and to help them develop their understanding of language. If you are introducing a word or phrase which is particularly difficult to come to terms with or which is hard to define through the use of other words, look for opportunities to point out examples of the meaning of the word. Here are five ways in which you might do this:

- Display one or more images on the board and point to these as examples of the word or phrase.
- Bring in some objects which you can point to as definitions of the word or phrase. If possible, bring in enough so that they can

be passed around the class, giving every student the opportunity to touch and hold them.
- Point to examples of the word or phrase which are in the classroom.
- Take students out of the classroom and find a place where you can point to a definition of the word or phrase. For example, if you were trying to teach the concept 'frustration', you might take students onto the school field (if you have one), stand beneath a tree which is taller than you are, attempt to reach a branch of the tree and then experience failure in this task again and again. This, you would say, was an example of frustration.
- Show a video which contains examples of the word or phrase. Point these out while pupils are watching; if appropriate, stop the film and discuss the examples with your class.

How does it differentiate?

- A linguistic definition of a word is highly abstract and relies on a sound understanding and detailed knowledge of the meaning of other words (those used to give the definition). An ostensive definition is concrete and empirical. It is therefore easier for all students to grasp.
- Giving concrete definitions of words through exemplification is a way of supporting less able students. They can be given in conjunction with traditional definitions. This will help pupils to contextualise and come to terms with the latter.
- Using media, objects or a journey outside the classroom is a good way of creating variety. As has been said elsewhere, this increase motivation, enthusiasm and engagement.

19. Analogies

What does it involve?

Analogies have already been mentioned in the earlier entry on exemplifying and explaining. However, they are such a useful tool for unlocking understanding that it is worth giving them a separate treatment here.

An analogy is a piece of reasoning in which similarity between separate items is identified and therefore used to make claims about these items. Here is an example:

'Society is like the human body. It possesses many different parts but these all work in unison to ensure the wellbeing of the overall structure. If there is a problem with one part, it affects everything. For example, if you get a bladder infection, the whole body suffers; if the education system stops working, all of society suffers.'

This is a classical analogy from Sociology. It is used by a group of thinkers called Functionalists as a means to describe how society works. It demonstrates the nature of analogies, their strengths and, also, their limitations.

One of the major strengths of using analogies is that you can explain an item (A) with which the audience may not be familiar, or of which they may have limited knowledge, by reference to another item (B) with which they are familiar, or of which they have greater knowledge. In the case above, the understanding of the human body most people possess is called on as a means to explain the Functionalist interpretation of society. In a sense, an analogy lays existing understanding on top of something new and, through pointing out similarities, helps the audience to understand that new item.

A major limitation of reasoning through similarity is that such an approach is likely to lead one to discount those things which do not fit the analogy. So, for example, in the Functionalist case outlined above, no consideration is given to those aspects of society which appear to be in regular, or perennial, conflict. These are ignored because they do not fit the analogy. Therefore, the explanatory power of the analogy is limited – if it is pushed too far, then the claims it makes start to look farcical and tendentious.

To conclude, analogies are a useful tool for the teacher but should not be pushed too far. Because they can help pupils to understand new items through reference to existing knowledge they are excellent for differentiating. In essence, they are a way of scaffolding thinking; a means by which to explain new, difficult or abstract concepts so that they can be grasped by pupils.

How does it differentiate?

- Analogies use the audience's existing knowledge to explain something new. Therefore, if analogies are carefully chosen, they can be used to help all students develop understanding.
- Analogies are a way of scaffolding thinking. This means that they lead students from what they already know to an understanding of something new.
- Analogies often provide clear and vivid images to explain abstract concepts. This helps pupils to come to terms with such ideas and to remember them.

20. Do the Word

What does it involve?

It has been demonstrated that multi-sensory experiences often lead to stronger and more vivid memories. A way in which to take advantage of this fact is by having students 'do' new words that they learn. Here are five examples to show what this might mean:

- **New word: Satisfaction.** The teacher stands at the front of the class and says the word 'satisfaction' out loud while displaying through their face and body what someone who is satisfied looks like. The class then stand up, face the teacher and repeat what they did – both the speaking of the word and the doing of the action. A series of ever more exaggerated displays of satisfaction could then follow, building up into a crescendo.
- **New word: Gravity.** Students work in pairs. Each pair is given a selection of small items of various weights. The teacher explains to the class that they are now scientists who have been asked to demonstrate gravity on television. First, the teacher does their own demonstration. This involves dropping an item from a few feet, pointing at the area in which it fell and declaring 'That's gravity!' Pairs then create their own demonstrations using their various items.
- **New word: Meander.** The class line up behind the teacher, who then moves off, meandering around the room. The line of students follows the teacher, mimicking what they do. The teacher might like to shout out lines such as: 'We're going on a meander!' or, 'This is a meander, we're winding from side to side.' Pupils could echo these lines in a game of call and response.
- **New word: Trans-national.** Students are asked to congregate on one side of the room. The teacher explains that every member of the class represents one employee of SuperBrains Incorporated, a trans-national company. They then read off a series of countries in which the company operates. As each

country is read off, a student is sent to a certain part of the room which represents that country. Pupils write their country on a piece of SuperBrains inc. branded paper and hold it up.

- **New word: Giraffe.** The teacher shows students a video of a giraffe and introduces the word. Pupils are then put into pairs and asked to play the part of a giraffe by working together. This will likely involve one pupils being the body of the giraffe and one pupil being the head and neck. 'Giraffes' then move around the room declaring that they are giraffes and shouting out the different features that giraffes possess.

Each of these examples tackles the concept of 'doing' new words slightly differently. In each case, a means has been devised to allow students to interact physically and verbally with one another in order to come to terms with the word in question. Play is used throughout. This allows pupils the opportunity to explore the new words, to practice using them and to develop some strong memories of their first experiences of them.

How does it differentiate?

- Multi-sensory activities increase the likelihood that all students in a class will be able to find a way of accessing the learning.
- Acting out words is an additional means of understanding their meaning. Some students may find visual and verbal explanation difficult to penetrate; doing words offers them another way of developing their understanding.
- Playing with new words gives pupils a chance to manipulate and explore their meaning and use. All students are included in such an activity because all students know how to play. It is also fund, which increase motivation and engagement.

Chapter Seven – Conclusion

So there you have it, one hundred strategies, activities and techniques helping you to differentiate in the classroom, no matter what age group or subject you teach.

Throughout the book, there have been some common themes:

- Differentiation involves having a range of methods at your disposal, with these being deployed as and when is appropriate, given the circumstances.
- Differentiation involves finding ways to ensure the whole class can make progress, regardless of individual starting points.
- Differentiation is closely linked to motivation and engagement.
- Differentiation involves stretching and challenging all pupils and giving everyone the opportunity to experience success.
- Differentiation involves teachers being flexible and responding to the needs of their students.

These five points are worth bearing in mind during the course of your teaching. Each offers a prism through which to view teaching and learning. You can use them to assess whether or not what is happening in your classroom is sufficiently differentiated. If you find the answer is 'no', you have the means to change things at your fingertips.

19842180R00109

Printed in Poland
by Amazon Fulfillment
Poland Sp. z o.o., Wrocław